Six When He Came to Us

A Memoir of International Adoption

Ellie Porte Parker

Celena,
   Enjoy!

Ellie Porter

First published by Dog Ear Publishing
4010 W. 86th Street, Ste H
Indianapolis, IN 46268
www.dogearpublishing.net

ISBN: 978-1-4575-1217-9

This book is printed on acid-free paper.

Printed in the United States of America

For Dmitry, Frank, Franklin,
and all the wonderful people
in my life who have shown me the
magic of love and connection

TABLE OF CONTENTS

ACKNOWLEDGEMENTS

I would like to thank the many people who read this book, made suggestions and helped me in so many ways. I especially want to thank Nancy Seid and Matt Witten for encouraging me to pursue this and for reading it endless times. My friends at the Creative Block and my writing group were all immensely helpful. Nancy Butcher Ohlin, John McPherson, Jeff Kelly, John DeDakis, Marsha Rosenblum, Sally Harder, Robin Eichen and Steven Malin all assisted me in various ways.

There were also many people who participated in making this story a happy one, including my sister Barbara Ann Porte who came to Russia with me and my friend Svetlana Gelfand who helped Dmitry and me communicate during his early time here. And of course, my husband, Frank, supported me in countless ways throughout the whole process.

INTRODUCTION

I have a vivid memory of leaving the orphanage in Russia with my son, Dima, dressed in his new American clothes, one hand holding mine, and the other clutching the toy lamb I'd brought along for him. He was six, old enough to know his whole world was about to change. I was wracked with worry, and wondered what the future would hold, but when I looked at his face, I knew he was even more anguished than I and that he was depending on me. I realized that I was all he had in the world and I swore to myself that I was going to be the best parent I could be, although I knew that that was no guarantee of a good ending. Even then, I knew the saga of international adoption was much more complicated than often anticipated.

During the time that Dima was growing up, the public perception changed from a belief that love would solve all problems for abandoned children, to a fear that any child who had spent significant time in an orphanage was irreparably damaged. Neither sentiment captures the true picture.

The social upheaval that existed in Eastern Europe during the early 1990s led to news reports of heartbreaking conditions in orphanages, resulting in large numbers of children being adopted internationally. Night after night, the media carried stories of children stranded in orphanages in desperate situations, and stories of children adopted by Americans who had rushed in to help. Emotional problems weren't being discussed much in the world of adoption, although there had been hints even during the mid-1900s that the ability of children to form attachments could be disrupted by traumatic early events. However, as more and more unexpected behavioral and emotional issues surfaced in internationally adopted children, these facts began to be known.

Still, when David Polreis died in 1996, the whole world of international adoption gasped. David was a two year old who had been adopted six months earlier from Russia, and was beaten to death by his distraught adoptive mother. The details of the case have been debated, but the general consensus in adoption circles is that David exhibited reactive attachment disorder, a disorder that more frequently occurs in children who have lived in orphanages and have not had the opportunity to bond with a caregiver, and that his adoptive mother was unable to deal with his behavior. Children with reactive attachment disorder engage in disruptive, and often violent, aggressive behaviors and try their caregiver's endurance sometimes to the breaking point.[1] David's death put the world on notice that the issues of international adoption could be more complicated than anyone imagined, and that children might have more than just the typical problems parents might expect. In the next fifteen years, fourteen more children adopted from Russia died in ways that involved their adoptive parents. Many of these children had severe behavioral problems.[2]

But older-child adoption does not equal attachment disorder.[3] There are older children who have been subjected to unthinkable neglect and abuse who are able to overcome their early lives, and there are individual differences in how resilient a child proves to be. Amid the stories of children with violent, aggressive behaviors, the stories of children who are able to surmount their early difficulties and thrive are often lost.

For every horrific story, there are thousands of other stories of adopted children who went on to connect with their new families and form part of the saga of the human story of coping, resilience and love.

Each story shows a small piece of the puzzle, and only by coming together, putting our pieces in the right place, and stepping back, will we understand the meaning of international adoption. My small corner of the world, my puzzle piece, shows my son Dima. And when I look at this section of the picture, I see a child who, with almost no nurturing in his early life, became a warm and empathetic adult. Although so much attention has now begun to be focused on the problems of children who have been unable to connect to their new families, the puzzle would not be complete without the children who have transcended their early traumas and have become loving, caring people.

The stories of these resilient children are complicated and interesting in their own right, for what they tell us about connection, and about the role of stress and love in our lives. There are individual variations in people's responses to the same experiences, and these individual differences may be present as early as birth.[1] Research has begun to evaluate the interaction of the environment with genetic factors and to look at physiological changes in the brain related to stress and adversity.

Before starting my rookie year as a mom, I'd worked as a psychologist with children and families, and because of this, I have often thought of our own family's experiences in terms of the interaction between brain, development, and behavior. While this book is a memoir of our family's early time together, it looks not only at our personal story but at the many sides of international adoption. Although Dima was affected by his early experiences in some subtle and sometimes unexpected ways, he was able to connect and bond to others despite the fact that he had lived his early years in clinics and orphanages. We know that we were fortunate, that many of the children who have led difficult early lives were not able to overcome these early events.

We are all a part of some cosmic adventure and there is something to be learned from our experiences collectively, some meaning to be gotten that transcends our individual journeys. It's in this intersection of adversity and coping that we can learn lessons about our humanity, about survival, and about hope. It was for this reason that I wanted to tell our story of connecting as a family.

CHAPTER 1

Choices

May you live through interesting times...

$\mathcal{S}$ ometimes, when I think about our adoption of Dima, I wonder how we got the courage to go through with it. Parenthood is terrifying enough under any circumstances, but adopting an older child from abroad can instill bone-chilling fear. My husband and I swore to love, care for, and cherish a person we did not yet know, and we swore to do this for the rest of our lives.

Dima came into my life by way of a telephone call. One afternoon when I picked up the phone, an incredibly high-pitched, young voice said, "Hello, my name is Allison, and I'm your adoption coordinator. You're on the top of my Russian List." The words hung there for a moment, suspended in time. Although my husband and I had applied to an adoption agency, our application had sunk into oblivion for months now, and until that moment I had no idea that I had an adoption coordinator or that I was on the top of any list, let alone a Russian one. The year was 1993 and the words "Russian List" only conjured up visions of James Bond movies for me. We had applied for international adoption almost accidentally; we wanted to adopt a child and my husband was over the age limit to qualify for many of the programs in this country. We had no idea that we were on a list to adopt from Russia, although it was a happy surprise, since my family roots stretch back to Odessa.

Allison continued talking at breakneck speed. I could swear I heard gum snap, but surely that is memory falsifying. She told me she had just gotten back from one of her many trips to Russia and began reeling off the names and descriptions of several children whom she was trying to place from there. The information she gave me was so unexpected, so out of context in this moment in my life, that I felt overwhelmed. I could hardly take in anything she was telling me.

Then she paused, rather dramatically, and said, "I would especially love to find a home for a little boy named Dima. Hey, how about I fax you a picture of him? You'll fall in love with him, I swear it. A woman I just arranged an adoption for saw this little guy when she went to Syktyvkar to pick up her baby and she absolutely fell in love with him and begged me to find him a family." Without missing a beat, Allison continued, "What's your fax number? Take a look and see what you think."

Somehow this wasn't how I anticipated this all working, but I gave her my fax number, switched on the fax machine and watched in astonishment as the black-and-white grainy picture emerged feet first through my machine, a breech birth of sorts. The child whose picture appeared looked uncannily familiar, a ringer in fact, for my sister, Barbara. He had dark, brooding eyes, and an intensity about him; he would fit right into our family of temperamental souls. In that moment, I felt in my heart that he would be mine.

I asked Allison to tell me what she could, and heard papers rustle as she went through his resume. It was long and sad for a child of only six. She told me he had been living in a series of children's clinics until he was four, because he'd had surgery for a hip problem, and after that was moved to the children's home in Syktyvkar, Russia. She stopped reading then, and said, "The head of the orphanage is desperate to get him out of the system there because she can't keep him after next month since he is already a year older than is allowed, and she'll have to send him on to another place. The other place is supposed to be pretty bad, and there are a lot of older, tougher kids there," she told me as pictures of Dickinsonian workhouses raced through my head. "She's worried he won't do well there, that it will change him. She says he's so kind and polite. He's only been able to stay at the home for young children as long as he has because of the surgery."

As I was mulling this over, considering the implications, Allison offered to send me a videotape of him. How could I say no, even though I knew that once I saw the videotape that would be it? I was already involved; the moment of conception had passed, as it were.

I told her to send the tape, and I would call her back as soon as my husband and I had looked at it. I hung up the phone and sat back on the couch considering this turn of events. I had wanted a child for a long time, but had never considered adopting one this age. All the warnings echoed in my ears. After all, a six year old is already his own person. And yet, the fact that he was already a person with his own ideas and thoughts lent a certain mystery and intrigue to him. I wondered who he would be, what stories and ideas he would bring with him.

My husband arrived home only a few minutes after I received the picture. I told him the story of Allison's phone call and showed him the faxed picture. Although my husband had accompanied me to the adoption agencies and dutifully filled out forms, I don't think the reality of adopting a child had really hit him until this moment.

He smiled down at the faxed picture. "He's a regular Mr. Sunshine, isn't he?" he asked cheerfully, looking at Dima's somber face. He paused, looked again at the picture, and said, without any prompting, "He looks just like your sister."

My husband and I first considered adoption shortly after we got married. I was thirty-five and he was forty-five. Although I had assumed that someday I would have a child, I had never before considered making motherhood the focus of my life. Sometimes I thought about a story I read in which the author described a party game. The game required each participant to describe his or her life, and the descriptions enabled the listener to gauge what was most important to the speaker. Women sometimes identified themselves first as a mother then gave other information. The author of the story said, with pride, that she always identified herself first by what she did, her vocation, her interests. I had thought about that comment often because, for a long time in my life, it seemed natural to identify myself in that way also. I would say I'm a graduate student, a psychologist, a potter, describing what I was doing at any given moment. But somewhere in time, my idea shifted. I felt that it was no truer to describe myself by explaining how I spent my time, than by explaining how I was connected to other people. I began to see relationships as important in telling the story of my life. The beauty and the music of connections to other people, to the universe, showed themselves to me. I began to hunger for different kinds of connections, and especially for motherhood.

But when we applied to adoption agencies, we discovered that once you are over forty your application gets metaphorically shifted from the "A" pile to the "B" pile. Would-be adoptive parents are plentiful in this country, and the agencies told us there are fifty parents waiting for every infant. We felt that surely there must be older children in need of a home, and we would rather adopt a child who might not otherwise have a home, than compete for a baby. In the end, we decided on a plan of overseas adoption, and began to hear of places we only barely knew existed before, places like Uzbekistan and Kazakhstan.

However, while we were waiting, many of the countries for which we had qualified closed their programs. Shortly after we applied, we got a telephone call from our agency telling us that we were not on any active list, information we received with a mixture of sorrow and relief.

So when we got the call from Allison that winter of 1993, when the breakup of the Soviet Union was well under way and hundreds of thousands of children were stranded in orphanages there, it was totally unexpected. A few months earlier,

Russian children with medical problems had begun to be available for international adoption, although we had not known about it. And apparently, we were on the list.

The videotape arrived the very next day after the phone call and that night my husband and I sat huddled together in the darkened room with only the light from the television set by which to see. The film flickered on, and the camera panned to an old white building, the children's home. Snow blanketed everything, and there was a pervasive feeling of isolation in the stark, white landscape. The plain painted wood exterior of the building was peeling in places, giving it a forlorn look. An army ambulance, parked outside the front door, was used to run errands and transport the children. The home was only two stories high and was dwarfed by the tall white apartment buildings that surrounded it. The snow and the icy climate apparently awed the narrator of the film. "Look at all the snow," the voice repeated time and again. Then the film switched to the inside of the orphanage.

Although the children's home was sparsely furnished, colorful murals had been painted on the walls, murals of American cartoon characters with a Russian look, Mickey Mouse with work boots, and circus characters out of the 1950s. Toys were visible, and several of the rooms, surprisingly, had beautiful rugs. One of the rooms held rows and rows of cribs. Babies were everywhere. There were babies being carried by stern looking women dressed in uniforms, babies playing on the floor, babies sitting on potties. The sound of crying was overwhelming.

But it was the women who held my attention. They all looked so sturdy and conscientious. They wore heavy stockings and oxfords. No one smiled. They were attending to the children, carrying them, changing them, and teaching them. I could tell just by looking at them that they had serious business to do with no time for nonsense. Each adult cared for 13 children.

After a few minutes, two older children, a boy and a girl, came into view. I knew the boy was Dima. I recognized him from the faded fax photo I'd gotten just the day before. In the fax picture he had been solemn and unsmiling. In the video he was smiling shyly, peeking carefully around the video camera, apparently asking questions in Russian about how it worked. He chewed gum gleefully. He had a small scar on his chin, which caught my attention. I wondered if I'd ever find out how he got it or about the other mysteries of his early life.

The little girl was Nadia, and she was definitely in charge. She had misshapen hands and an eye that didn't focus. She had to tilt her head to see but she observed the world shrewdly. Several of her fingers had been amputated, for what reason I would never know. "Probably from frostbite," the director would tell me. Later I found out Nadia's version. She told Dima she was so bad that someone must have chopped them off. She would whisper this and other stories to him in the dark of night, and Dima would believe them.

More glimpses of two children running, exploring, peeking in a mirror appeared. Then the film flickered off.

I found myself torn about taking this next step, a step that would change everything. I wished desperately I could peek into the future and see how things would turn out. My life now flowed from one day to the next, not unhappily. I had sisters, a husband, and work. And yet, although I was not discontent, I yearned for something more, some connection, some idea of parenthood, fuzzily defined.

But there was no way to know beforehand who this child really was, and no way to know what kind of mother I would be to him. This was to be my first, long awaited child, although my husband had three children, two of whom were grown. The youngest one, Franklin, didn't yet live with us. Although I had wanted to have or adopt a child for years, the child in my unarticulated, ill-defined dreams had been young and malleable, not a real and separate entity. I was worried, but somehow very touched by Allison's story of Dima and by my glimpses of the little boy on the tape.

After having been closed out of program after program because of age, we empathized with this little guy who at age six was considered to be too old to have a future or a family. Just as forty was at that time the magic barrier for becoming parents, five seemed to be the barrier for getting your family if you were a child. Dima and my husband and I had this in common: we'd all crossed into the no-man's land of the adoption world.

My husband and I kept replaying the video, watching it over and over, as if we could wrest some clues from it that were not immediately forthcoming. The one thing that scared us both was the thought of adopting a child with significant emotional problems, a child who couldn't attach to us.

I called Allison. He was adorable, I assured her. But I wished I could have more information, wondered what else she could tell me. Allison seemed perplexed by my hesitation. She told me how her parents had just adopted two children, a boy and a girl, three and five. They couldn't bear to leave those children there, she told me, as though I should have that same attitude. All the children she had placed were doing well. She didn't have any other information to give me, no developmental records or medical records, but her tone clearly implied I shouldn't need them. However, just before she hung up, she suggested that perhaps I could call the pediatrician at the children's home since he spoke a bit of English and knew all the children.

I called the children's home in Russia. The pediatrician spoke willingly to me, but his English was minimal. He told me he did not know Dima well, but that he seemed to be a "very bright, alert child, and so polite and kind."

Then I asked him if Dima wanted to be adopted and there was a pause. I felt that the question surprised the pediatrician, caught him off guard. He assured me that of course Dima wanted to be adopted; all the children wanted that. It seemed impossible to discuss this further. Later, my good Russian friend would tell me that in Russia children are simply expected to obey, that Russians don't discuss everything to death with their children as Americans do.

"In Russia," she would explain, "if the children must go to the doctor, we simply say, 'come get dressed, put on your coat, we must go some place.' Here, you tell them a week before, you show them pictures of the doctor's office, you tell them what the doctor will do, all these unnecessary things. They are children; they must do what they are told to do."

When I considered my conversation with the pediatrician, I realized it was the second time I heard the exact same words, "polite and kind," used to describe Dima. They were the words that helped me make up my mind, the words that initially connected us. The description of Dima as a kind person, his shy smile on the videotape, and even the fact that he was coming from Russia beckoned to me.

My grandparents came from Russia, and my father was born there. It had always seemed to me a country of awe and mystery, a country with secrets to tell. I felt as though I were exploring my own roots, roots that went back in this country to the early part of the century and stretched out to Eastern Europe before that. I could never resist the stories I heard as a child about my family coming to America as immigrants, struggling to stay alive; I could never resist the mysteries they unlocked. Stories told through the medium of a different culture, the angles skewed just a little, make you understand things in a different way. Perhaps the fact that Dima would come with stories all his own intrigued me.

And yet, I knew things about adopting older children that made me shudder. I knew that children in orphanages were at higher risk for a variety of developmental problems, and I knew about the children in orphanages who failed to thrive even when all their physical needs were met, when they had food and medical care. I knew that babies died lacking only for love, for connection.

The history of adoption is made up of individual stories that range from broken connections that are never healed, to connections forged with love so fierce it defies understanding.

Humans are designed to form bonds, connections of intimacy. In the 1930s people had thought physical care was enough, that warmth and food were all that babies required. Babies in institutions were handled efficiently, but without cuddling, without emotional nurturing. Everything was done on schedule, but with as little human contact as possible. And when the babies began to die, the researchers moved in with their theories and tried to understand the importance, the meaning of bonding and attachment between baby and adult, between mother and child.[5] They began to consider the importance of touch and nurturing. I had studied child development for years, had a doctorate in the field. I knew the general wisdom was that babies deprived of love in the first few months of life would be irreparably affected. Somehow though, in the 1990s those cautionary studies had been forgotten in the adoption world.

But still, Allison's description, especially the words "kind and polite," echoed through my head, as I replayed the tape. Dima seemed like a survivor to me, and I knew that adopting a younger child would be no guarantee of anything. Adopting an older child at least had the advantage of being able to catch a glimpse of who the child was destined to be. Many of the developmental problems of institutionalized children show up well before age five, and the fact that he was doing well where he was, was a good sign. My husband felt that Dima was an empathetic, caring person caught in a terrible situation.

When I called Allison and told her we wanted to adopt Dima, she said I needed to be there in ten days. When I gasped audibly, she conceded that this seemed like short notice. But, she explained, the whole process was set up in advance, and there was an open slot for another set of adoptive parents in ten days. Either we would be there, or someone else would fill the slot.

The idea of leaving everything in my life and traveling to Russia in that short a time span seemed inconceivable to me. Not only was ten days an impossibly short time in which to finish up paperwork, arrange a leave of absence from my job and obtain a visa, but it gave me no time to sort things through emotionally. I'm the kind of person who needs more than ten days to decide if I want to buy a new dress. I finally told her that I thought I could get everything ready in four weeks, but ten days just wasn't possible. She sighed, and told me she would call her overseas coordinators and see what she could do.

It turned out that she couldn't do anything. If we wanted to wait more than ten days, she'd keep us on her list, but we would be starting over, and she couldn't guarantee anything. She didn't know if the same child or even the same geographical location would be available. And of course, the political situation was so unstable that no one ever knew when the whole process would close. The Soviet Union was in political turmoil at that time, with hints of possible revolution under the surface.

I agreed to get there in ten days; I was committed now and couldn't just leave him there. Before I hung up the telephone, Allison told me she had some additional tasks for me. I needed to shop for presents to give to people in Russia, and I needed to shop for clothes for Dima, since all his clothing would be given to the next child. In Russia, gift giving was considered polite. Allison explained that I mustn't think of it as a bribe because it wasn't. You don't give a gift to get someone to do something for you, she explained; you give the person a gift after they've done something for you, to thank them for their kindness.

Allison faxed me a list of suggested gifts. I must get something very special for the head of the children's home, perhaps a leather handbag or something of that nature, and scarves and calculators made good gifts for other people who did special favors. She also suggested I bring cartons of cigarettes and several American T-shirts to hand out in appreciation of more routine favors. I needed to get a week's worth of clothes for Dima in addition to a winter jacket, a hat, gloves, boots, and a scarf. She further suggested that I put together a small album containing pictures of our home and family members. I would need to show it to officials in Russia to reassure them that Dima was going to a good home and it would also be useful to show to Dima.

My husband and I discussed how we could divide up the tasks we had ahead us to get ready for our new child in such a short time. We decided that the only way things could work was if my husband stayed home and set things up as best he could here, while I went without him to Russia. We both decided I should have someone else come along and my sister

Barbara, who lives in Virginia, seemed like a logical choice. She's a writer so her schedule is flexible, and of course, being a sister gives her a pre-emptive edge. My other sister had a full time job with regular hours, so that didn't bode as well. I called Barbara and begged her to come. A trip to Russia is hard to squeeze into a "to-do list" for the following week.

"Being a writer and working at home is not the same as not working," she said. "Anyway, have you lost your mind? Russia, in ten days?"

"Think of how interesting it will be," I said.

"*'May you live through interesting times'* is an old Chinese curse," she replied.

But she agreed to accompany me, mostly because she loves me, but I think also because she, too, is a collector of stories, and I think the idea of seeing Russia intrigued her.

The sheer push to get everything done left little time for reflection, doubts, or long good-byes. And in exactly ten days after my initial conversation with Allison, my sister and I sat side by side in a FinnAir jet headed to Moscow.

CHAPTER 2

Outside Looking In

In her book Lost and Found: The Adoption Experience, Betty Jean Lifton[6] wrote of adoption, "Whether in fantasy or reality, it haunts us all, adopted and non-adopted alike. It is a metaphor for the human condition, sending us forth on that mythic quest that will prove that we are bonded to each other and to all the creatures of this world-and in the process, reveal to us who we are."

*T*he safe, cheery feeling ended abruptly, once the plane landed and we left the FinnAir jet. I felt as if we had ventured into another world through a time warp; the lights were dim, giving everything a dingy, worn look. Few people were around, and the airport seemed desolate, reminiscent of a scene in a science fiction movie in which the enemy has already struck, and the main characters find themselves in an eerily quiet place with no life forms. We looked around, not sure what we would find or what to do next.

Representatives from the adoption agency were supposed to meet us and take us to the home of a woman named

Zina, but we had been warned that in Russia plans often go awry. Suddenly, two young men, both in their twenties, appeared out of the shadows. They introduced themselves as Sergei and Sasha. Sergei was to be our translator. Sasha was a friend of Sergei's and had been recruited for this trip because he had a car. Although both were handsome, polite, and charming, they had a grim look that was to become familiar. Their jackets were brown, their hats were brown. I came to realize there were almost no colors in the clothing in Russia. There were no bright ski jackets, no red mittens nor red caps. The overall effect was that everything, everywhere, seemed muted and barely alive.

We got our first glimpse of Russian life on our ride from the airport to Zina's apartment. Sasha's car, into which we were all packed, was small and looked like a survivor of a demolition derby. It was borrowed from his father, he told us, and it was clear that Sasha was proud to have access to any vehicle. Automobiles were hard to come by in Russia in 1993.

About five minutes into our ride, a uniformed policeman pulled us over. The policeman and Sasha talked loudly for a few minutes, and Sasha gave him some money and got back in the car, slamming the door. He talked loudly to Sergei who explained to us that because of the dents, the police pulled Sasha over and asked if he had been in an accident, implying that perhaps someone had been hurt and that he had failed to report it. Sasha gave them money to let us go on without a fuss. This had happened to Sasha before. It was to happen four more times on that short trip to Zina's apartment. My sister leaned over and whispered, "It really pays to keep your car looking good here." In Russia, it was the details of everyday living that could wear you down.

Sergei, whose English was excellent, took care of everything, from the paperwork to the living arrangements, while we were in Russia. When we arrived at Zina's apartment she greeted us warmly in fluent English. She welcomed us into her apartment where she lived with her mother and her teenage daughter, Katia. Zina looked to be in her late thirties or early forties, and dressed in modest but fashionable Russian business attire, with a sleek suit and sensible low pumps.

She turned out to be a busy lady who not only rented out rooms in her apartment, but also worked as a translator by day, tutored children at night, and acted as a tour guide on weekends. Her mother, the babushka, did the housekeeping, stood in all the lines Russians seemed to need to stand in to get everyday items such as food, cooked the meals, and helped with all the guests. With all the changes in Russia, everyone was scrambling to make do.

The ever-efficient Allison had presented me with a list of appropriate presents to give them and so I had a pair of red shorts tucked in my suitcase for Katia and a package containing aluminum foil and toothpaste for Zina. Allison didn't miss much.

"Forget the lipstick and perfume. She's got drawers full of that stuff," Allison had advised me, when I proffered suggestions of gifts. "What she wants is all that stuff she can't get over there: instant coffee, aluminum foil, peanut butter."

I had added those to my shopping list.

Zina's apartment turned out to be beautiful inside, despite a shabby exterior. We stood in the vestibule, still in our boots, peeking in hesitantly. I saw shelves and shelves of books and a Baby Grand piano. I felt as though I had seen this place before, in a dream perhaps. Then I realized that there was something about the decor, the books, and the pictures that reminded me of my childhood home.

Zina came out and welcomed us, kindly, almost shyly. She motioned to us to take off our shoes and come into the apartment. In flawless English she told us how excited she was that we were there. It wasn't every day that Russian families had guests from America. But in the new Russia, with foreigners pouring into the country as though a dam had broken upstream and the water surged forth, even quiet Russian families were swept into the churning stream. Zina's daughter, Katia, and Zina's mother, both of whom lived in the apartment, came in to peek at us.

Babushka, the name we all used for Zina's mother, looked exactly like my image of a Russian grandmother. She was plump, with gray hair, always wore an apron, and spoke in a kind, soothing voice. She looked as though nothing in life could surprise her, as though she'd seen it all. All except, perhaps, people coming from halfway across the world to pluck a child out of an orphanage to take home with them. A robin, after all, sits on the eggs in its own nest but doesn't fly to the blue jays nest and return with its eggs. Nature has a plan, and all the creatures in that plan seem to understand it, except of course, for those crazy Americans.

But still, Babushka was solicitous of us. We might be crazy, but we had good hearts, and more importantly, we were in her charge. She and Zina both fussed over us constantly. They made sure we wore our gloves outside, and they both shook their heads sadly over the fact that I had no hat. In Moscow I could, perhaps, get by without one. But, Babushka thought, I must get one before I left for Syktyvkar. "Syktyvkar," she muttered and made shivering motions. It was decided, that the next day, Zina and Katia would take my sister and me to the open-air market where I could buy a hat.

We had arrived on a Sunday in Moscow, and that Monday was International Women's Day, a day on which all work stops in Russia. Women's Day is celebrated seriously in Russia, somewhat analogous to the way Mother's Day is celebrated in the United States, but it is more generous in the boundaries of appreciation of women. All women - girlfriends, wives, and friends - are honored, whether or not they are mothers. Women are given flowers or little gifts; they are shown appreciation for all the work that they do. Since it was impossible for us to pursue our adoption mission on that Monday, impossible to begin our work at the embassy, the "free market" was a good place to go.

This market was a new development in Russia, a large, open-air market where private vendors hawked their wares. Despite the gray, slushy snow on the ground, the entrepreneurs were out in force. Rows and rows of booths displayed hand painted jewelry, bowls and spoons and *matrioshka* dolls decorated in Russian folk art style with red, green and black lacquer.

My sister and I were instantly recognizable in this crowd as foreigners; our expressions, our haircuts, our makeup and our colorful coats and scarves screamed "American." We were especially coveted as customers because dollars were much preferred to rubles, which declined alarmingly in value day-by-day, even hour-by-hour, during our stay. The merchants called out to us, showed us their crafts and tried to woo us over to their stands. Most items sold for a few American dollars each, an amount equivalent to about a week's pay in Russia. A few dollars could purchase huge amounts of Russian food or clothes, or more recklessly, some little luxury so hard for Russians to find in Russia just then. In America, the equivalent would purchase a sandwich and a coke.

My mission here was to buy a warm hat, preferably a Russian style hat that would make me appear less foreign, and more a part of the crowd. Hats were selling in the market for about twenty-five American dollars, a huge amount of money for Russians. I examined several and tried one on, peeking in the mirror nearby to see if it transformed me. When several of the merchants saw me trying on the hat, they started to gather around us. They asked Katia about us, tried to gauge our sincerity. Once they knew we absolutely intended to buy a hat, (we heard the word Syktyvkar passing from mouth to mouth, saw the accompanying shivering motions), the competition for our business really heated up.

One young entrepreneur, who decided it was to be his sale no matter what, leaned over and whispered to Katia that he would slip her several dollars if she could talk us into buying a hat from him. It was Katia's first experience with the concept of the "kickback." I'm sure it was not her last. This man, intent on making the sale, helped me try on hat after hat, surveyed me from different angles, got his friends to select more hats and to offer opinions on the most flattering ones. Soon much of the market place had become involved; everyone was standing around pointing, giving nods of approval or shaking their heads, muttering *da* or *nyet*. Business had come to a standstill while I selected my hat. I finally chose one, a warm looking Russian-style fur hat that sat jauntily on my head, and the crowd cheered! I felt so connected to everyone here.

We returned to Zina's apartment to wait until we could leave for Syktyvkar. I had to prepare a myriad of paperwork at the embassy and schedule an exit interview. After all the adoption papers were complete, the last step a family had to complete was to go to the embassy, with the child and meet with an interviewer who presumably would give final approval if everything seemed in order.

Then finally, on Wednesday, Sergei told us we were ready to leave. We had only been there for four days but it felt as though we had left our American life far behind us months ago. We were beginning to feel as though Zina and her family were our family. They made meals for us, which included spaghetti for breakfast and they fussed over us. We would be returning to them soon, but now it was time to leave. Sergei brought along a new companion for the trip, Alex. Alex was older, perhaps 45, and looked like a caricature of an old-line Communist party member. He had thinning hair, a gold tooth, and a skinny tie. Although they were assigned to us by my adoption agency, ostensibly as translators, we always had the feeling that their job extended well beyond that. Sergei and Alex made sure we brought every scrap of paper we needed, stood in lines to file the endless paperwork. We had been instructed to take thousands of dollars with us in cash, which at the time was an ungodly amount of money in Russia, for travel expenses and overseas adoption fees, so I am sure they also served as unofficial bodyguards.

Sergei and Alex, true to their word, had taken care of everything for the trip. They purchased the plane tickets, drove us to the airport and even accompanied us. We had only to follow along, only to bring official papers and money. It was hard to believe that it had been only a little more than ten days since I had gotten that phone call from Allison.

By the time we got to the airport, it was midnight and the wind was howling. Alex and Sergei retreated to one corner of the waiting area, and my sister and I stood together silently, listening to the wind. Finally I put my hand in my coat pocket and drew out the faxed picture of Dima that I had gotten the day that Allison first called. I looked down at the wrinkled black-and-white photo showing a very solemn boy of about five or six years of age, standing stiffly by a telephone and I asked, "What do you think he'll be like?"

My sister shrugged indicating that it was impossible to know that; there was nothing she could tell me. I put the picture back in my pocket. Sergei and Alex came up to tell us it was almost time to go. They both carried what turned out to be vodka and beer in brown bags, to tide themselves over on the plane ride. While this behavior might be suspect in the United States, it appeared to be the norm in Russia. I discovered after we boarded the plane that my sister and I were probably the only two passengers not carrying a brown bag with us. But then, we weren't Russians, prepared for the harrowing plane rides often typical of the Russian airline, Aeroflot. We settled in and tried not to think about the frequent fuel shortages that plagued plane trips here.

I assumed that when our plane finally landed in Syktyvkar in the dark of night, we would go quietly to our hotel room. At home, I lived a quiet life; I was not treated to special courtesies nor was I the object of intense curiosity. It never occurred to me that here, in Syktyvkar, I had almost mythic status as an American coming to adopt a child for some inexplicable reason. In Russia, at the time, people rarely adopted children; children available for adoption were plentiful, and adoption was only talked about in hushed voices. Often, I was told, when a couple adopted a child they pretended the woman was pregnant, going so far as to stuff pillows in her clothing. Children who are adopted are often not told until they are adults, if then.

A Russian friend told me the story of an obstetrician who adopted a child he had delivered. The mother died during the birth, and no other family came forward to claim the child. The obstetrician could not bear to send her on to an orphanage, and to betray the trust he felt as he held her. Although the obstetrician was Caucasian and the child was Tartar in background, and looked very different from the doctor's family, he never told her that she was adopted. When she asked why she looked so different, the family shushed her and told her she looked like her great-grandmother. Only when she was an adult and after her parents had died did she discover the truth, but by then it was too late. The pieces of her life were confused. She could make little sense of who she was. "She died by her own hand," my friend had whispered. So given this context, the motives of a woman coming thousands of miles to adopt a six-year-old child must have seemed unfathomable. Any woman traveling so far must be rich and crazy, a combination sure to pique the interests of everyone. When we got off the plane, both the director of the orphanage and the head nurse were waiting to greet us. They were solid looking women in their mid-forties bundled up warmly and wearing Russian style fur hats on that very cold March night. They had probably left their warm homes and their families in the middle of the night to stand here in the freezing cold, a sure sign that we were very important people, visiting dignitaries, celebrities of a sort. The director of the orphanage, a woman named Galina, looked exhausted, as though she had gathered all her inner resources to make this trip, but her companion, Tatiana looked thrilled. She was absolutely effusive, although she didn't speak a word of English, and I didn't speak a word of Russian.

Sergei leaned over and whispered, "She is so excited that you saw a video tape of Dima and came all this way to adopt him. Such a romantic story," he said. Tatiana smiled broadly. I smiled back. There was nothing to say. It was impossible to describe in a few short sentences the complex series of events that had brought me there.

Still, I had no information about Dima, no medical records, nothing but my faxed photograph. I was hoping to get some more information that night, but it was not to be. In retrospect, I believe that the adoption bureaucracy in Russia preferred to show prospective parents their adorable children-to-be rather than scaring them off with dire sounding medical reports and case histories. Our meeting was limited to warm smiles. It was clear that Tatiana and Galina thought we were crazy, but nevertheless deserving of special treatment. And of course, they were thrilled that I was there to adopt Dima, to provide something better for one of their favorite children than what they had to offer him.

After we waved goodnight to Galina and Tatiana, Sergei and Alex whisked us away to our hotel room. They made sure we had anything we wanted, hoped the small comforts and special foods would make us feel at home. My sister fell asleep immediately, but I lay awake for hours it seemed, wondering if I was doing the right thing. I wasn't used to taking such irrevocable steps with so little information. I could not call out of the hotel and talk to my husband as I could in Moscow, and I desperately wanted his assurance, his cheerful optimism.

I thought about my mother that night and about how much I wished she were alive, right then, to share this. I knew my mother would have felt drawn into this story, and I knew the stories of her own childhood had influenced my feelings about adoption. Her childhood had been difficult after her father had died when she was only three years old.

My mother's parents had immigrated to the United States from the Polish-Russian area just before my mother was born. My grandfather started a roofing business in Brooklyn that was becoming quite successful. But then, he died suddenly in a terrible and famous accident when some scaffolding came down, and he fell to the ground, a workman on top of him.

My grandmother, who never became proficient in English, had five children by then, my mother the second from the youngest. My grandmother was left to raise the children herself in the early 1900s when there was little in the way of financial assistance. Relatives suggested that she put the children in an orphanage, or at least put the two youngest ones, my mother and her brother Harry, there. That way she could work during the day since the older three were already in school. In desperation, my grandmother considered this, but finally she decided to lease a low-rent tenement complex and operate it so she could keep all the children. She found one in Brooklyn and all six moved in. It was a difficult existence, but for my mother, the sorrow of her childhood lay not in the inconveniences or poverty, but in the fact that she didn't have a father. She keenly felt this loss and spoke of it often to me.

At the end of each workday, the fathers of the other children who lived in the apartment house returned home, often bringing with them some sweets or a penny for some candy.

Their arrival was an exciting moment each day for the other children, but a moment of disappointment for my mother. She had no father, and could only stand and watch as the other children climbed all over their daddies and got their hugs and treats. But the father of her best friend, Gertie, noticed that my mother and her younger brother hung sadly back in the hall when the other children got treats. He began to bring candy for them as well as for his own children, and my mother pretended he was her father, sometimes even pointed him out as such to other children. The stories of my mother's narrow escape from life in a children's home, and her fatherless childhood made more bearable by the kindness of Gertie's father, were a part of the fabric of my childhood.

And when I thought about Dima, saw his situation in light of my own background, I knew why I had felt pulled in to his story, pulled into it as though it was a natural extension of my family story. If we wanted to add a child to our lives, who better than Dima, a child who clearly needed a family, a child who brought me full circle to my family's roots, who despite enormous odds and a difficult beginning, thought enough of others to show kindness and empathy. Finally, with those thoughts in mind, I fell asleep.

My sister and I awoke early the next morning and prepared to go down to the children's home. The details of the morning seemed maddening. I could think only of meeting Dima, and yet I had to get dressed, eat breakfast, smile at my sister, at Sergei and Alex. Finally, we left for the children's home.

Sergei and Alex gallantly guided us through the streets and hailed a car over to where we were standing. We climbed in, only to find that there was no meter, no picture of the driver. This was not a taxi; we had hitched a ride. As always, in Russia, money changed hands. My sister and I exchanged glances as if to say, our fate is not in our own hands now, we can only hope for the best.

We arrived at the children's home, my heart beating hard in anticipation and fear. I had seen glimpses of the home in the videotape, but still, I wondered what I would find. And of course, I wondered what Dima would be like.

But as we entered the building, we could see that it was clean, that people had tried their best to make it cheerful. A faint odor of urine mixed in with the odor of disinfectant greeted us, a reminder, after all, that there were ninety children, most of them babies, living under one roof.

"Come," said Galina, "you will meet Dima. The children have just come into the activity room, and you can play with him there."

The first time I saw Dima, he was standing shyly in the corner, looking very displeased. Earlier that morning the children had been told that a mother was coming. It was an exciting event, spoken about in whispers and giggles. However, when Dima learned it was his mother who had arrived, he did not greet this announcement with unmitigated joy. I assumed that even though he was told this was a new mother, he still had a few issues to take up with any mother of his, new or old for that matter. Why, for instance, he would want to know, had he been left so long in this place? Old hurts are not easily forgiven.

However, despite his reservations, Galena told me that Dima had talked about his mother coming for him for quite some time, and although he'd never met her, he felt connected to her. I'm sure he thought that she would speak Russian with a lilt and have a beautiful smile and would reach down and take his hand and lead him home, away from this crowded noisy place. But as soon as Dima heard me speak he must have known that I was the wrong mother, that I wasn't anything like the mother he had dreamed about.

That morning he pleaded, "Please listen! There must be a mistake. My mother speaks Russian."

He was terribly upset when Tatiana told him, "This is your new mother, and you will go home to America with her." He later told me that he had envisioned going off with a wonderful Russian family, living close to the place he was now, perhaps seeing the children from the children's home now and then, having them admire his warm, comfortable home life. But now they were trying to foist off on him a woman obviously too stupid even to speak Russian.

"Well sure, I wanted a better life for myself, but I never thought that I'd have to go that far, or learn a whole new language. I just thought I'd get a nice family nearby," he said when we discussed it when he was older.

But as usual, no one had listened to him, and so he stood quietly sulking in the corner of the room. The adults all told me he was just shy. But later, when I knew him, I understood that this was the pose he went into when he was furious. Finally one of the staff went over to Dima again, to coax him out of the corner. The staff member pointed to me, encouragingly, but Dima hung ragdoll limp and refused to look at me. All the adults chucked him under the chin and chided him. In retrospect, Dima's attitude was actually a good sign. It's normal for children to be wary of strangers, especially strangers who don't speak their language and indicate they are going to take them far away.

Although I had been worried about meeting Dima, worried about what he would be like, I hadn't really been concerned about what he would think of me. I had heard stories about how excited children were when potential parents came to the children's homes, how they all clamored for attention. And I had worked with children for years, and usually found it easy to get them to join with me in play.

At first I tried to get him interested in playing with some toys, but he remained aloof and clearly would have nothing to do with me. My sister whispered, "I think it's a good sign that he won't go with just anyone."

I knew that, in a way, she was right. Indiscriminate friendliness is sometimes a sign of trouble. Children with attachment disorders are often initially overly friendly.

"I think you're right," I answered, "but still, it would be nice if he didn't seem to hate me. What if he never gets to like me?"

My sister leaned over and said, "Don't be silly, of course he'll like you. He'll love you; you're his mother!"

I wasn't sure this was at all true. However, I didn't have much of a chance to think about it because the other children quickly surrounded me. Even if Dima was not thrilled to see me, everyone else was clearly in a state of excitement. An adorable little boy raced over to me with a huge ball and flung it in my direction, laughing gleefully, attempting to entice me to play. He looked to be about two or three years of age. The director smiled down at him and put her hand on his head, saying, "Ah, this one, we got him only last month. There are no health problems. He will go to a Russian family. Can you imagine, he was found wandering around the airport with a note from the mother pinned to the jacket. It said, 'Please take care of my child. I cannot feed him anymore. He will starve if I keep him.' " The director looked resigned. "The economy, it is so bad," she sighed.

I swallowed hard, realizing all at once that to be able to take care of a child was to be privileged, blessed. For the first time I truly understood that each child in this room arrived here because of someone's hardship and sorrow, and each child was totally alone in the world.

I was thinking of this when a little girl rushed up to me and crawled into my lap. I recognized her from the videotape as Nadia. She was easy to spot with her crossed eyes and misshapen hands. But what was more apparent, when meeting her, was her charisma. It was impossible not to be charmed by her. She was obviously intelligent, and she smiled up at me and cuddled closely into my lap. She talked rapidly and earnestly to me in Russian. The fact that the hands she twined around me were misshapen somehow endeared her to me even more because it made clear her courage in the face of daunting odds.

"What is she saying?" I asked Sergei, our translator.

Sergei looked uneasy. "She says, 'Take me home to America.'" He turned away from me and explained to the little girl, in Russian, that this was to be Dima's mother. The girl said something to him, and he smiled sadly and shrugged his shoulders. I looked quizzically at him wanting to know what she had said.

"She asks, 'When will it be my turn to go to America?' And of course, I have no answer for her." Nadia had a realistic assessment of her situation. No one was coming for her. The orphanage was bad. A home in America was good. Period. Nadia's story haunts me still.

I glanced at Dima, who was still standing in the corner, and decided my best approach was to play with the other children, to get him to be interested in me. I ignored him and played catch with a group of children. I also spun some of the hula-hoops with great skill, something I had mastered in my childhood in the 1950s. Dima continued to hang back and watch me from the corner of his eye, unready to commit himself. However, I did notice a little smile creeping onto his face, and he began to show some interest. Finally, the director came over and said, "You know, Dima is so shy, and he feels everything inside him so deep, maybe it would be best to take him by himself into another room and get to know him a little bit."

Tatiana, the pretty woman with a big smile I had met the night before, took Dima by the hand and led him to the gymnasium. She knew him well since she was the one who went with him to get his medical checkups, the one who took him for his eye evaluations and helped him choose his glasses with the little red frames. He was not wearing those glasses when I saw him, and I did not find out that he even had glasses until several days later. They were stuffed away in one of his pockets, perhaps all the better to make a first impression.

Tatiana waved goodbye and left us alone in the gymnasium. We had hoops and balls but no common language. Dima eyed me somewhat suspiciously. He wasn't used to having an adult all to himself, and this had some possibilities, even if I were exceptionally inept. For lack of anything else to do, I started throwing a ball to him. It was as though he suddenly came alive, as though this was the magic action he needed. He had never had an opportunity, as far as I could tell, to play ball with a grown-up all by himself and he laughed out loud and jumped with excitement.

Maybe I could get him to like me after all, I thought. Encouraged by his wonderful smile, I tried even harder. I began to notice more about him, how he had a certain dignity and a certain warmth. I began to feel connected to him as we stood there playing catch. Neither of us wanted to be the first to stop throwing the ball, since it was unclear what else we could do together, but I could throw a ball only so many times. I put the ball down and took out a small flashlight my sister had given me. I pointed it toward the wall and showed Dima how to use his hands to make shadow figures, at first a duck, then a wolf and a cat. Other fearsome creatures soon followed. He was very good at imitating my hand positions and was soon able to make the animals himself.

"*Yo sem*," he said solemnly. It means "myself" (as in "I'll do it myself and I don't need you to help me") and was a phrase I would hear very often in the months to come. He then showed me he could make other animals by this shadow method, and we chased each other's hands around and barked aggressively and laughed.

I soon exhausted all the possibilities of games I could think of to play with no common language, and I cast around for something new to do. I remembered a book I had brought from the United States and showed it to Dima. He was immediately interested, and we sat down on one of the mats. He snuggled right next to me and smiled shyly at me. The book had colorful pictures of everyday objects, and I had hoped to use it to help in communication. I thought that if he was hungry he could point to food; if he wanted to play, he could point to toys. Looking back at this, I realize how naive I was about the complexities of communication.

The translator soon came into the room to tell me it was time for Dima to go back to his group and for me to meet again with Galina. Dima held up the book that we had been looking at and pointed urgently at it while talking to Sergei.

Sergei laughed. "He says your book is very nice. He wishes he had such a book."

"Tell him it's his," I said eagerly. I was anxious to score some points with Dima. "I brought it for him." To prove the point, I took out a pen and said, "Here, we will write his name in the book for him." I realized all of a sudden that I didn't know how to spell his name. I started to write it the way it sounded to me. "Demar," I said.

"No, no 'r' in it" said Sergei. So I wrote in the front, "This book belongs to Dema."

Dima watched intently as I did this, looking very excited. I asked if he wanted to write his name in Russian, and Sergei translated. Dima shook his head. He was too tired to do so, he told Sergei. The translator informed me that Dima had not yet been to school and was a bit self conscious that he didn't know his letters, although of course he'd had no opportunity to learn them. I felt badly that I had embarrassed him. I finished writing 'Dema.' The translator looked a little uneasy. Then he said, "Actually the name is spelled 'Dima', it comes from the name 'Dmitry'." I sighed. I thought about the stories of my relatives who had had their names changed and mangled at Ellis Island, and there I was - a name mangler. But I gave the book to Dima, who was thrilled anyway. In that minute I realized I was about to bring a child thousands of miles across the sea, totally change his life and mine, and I didn't even know how to spell his name. I didn't even know it was short for Dmitry.

Galina came in just then, and Dima showed her the book excitedly. She smiled politely and explained that she would hold the book for Dima until tomorrow, when he would leave with me. Children were not allowed to have personal property except for their two sets of clothes. She explained that toys and books were usually kept together for everyone to share, and it would only make trouble, make the other children jealous, if Dima were allowed to bring the book back with him to his dormitory room. But she told Dima that the book was his, and that he would be able to take it with him when he left with his new mama. He smiled, seeming very satisfied with this turn of events, and left to go back to his group.

I headed to Galina's office for a meeting, where I was to get medical information and background. I was anxious, exhausted, stressed and still in possession of very little concrete information about Dima as I stood outside of the door of Galina's little office. I was relying on Galina to tell me what she knew of Dima's life up to that point.

CHAPTER 3

But He Can Walk Now

What happens in the first few years of life has a profound influence on how the brain develops. The child's experiences determine which neural pathways will be strengthened and which will disappear. There appear to be "sensitive" periods in brain development, the time during which it is possible for certain pathways to develop.[7] For example, in order for sight to develop, the eye needs to receive light during the first few weeks after birth. Kittens that aren't exposed to light the first four weeks of life will be permanently blind because the neurons in the brain didn't develop in response to light.[8] Language in particular appears to be a time sensitive skill.

We were crowded together, Galina, Tatiana, my sister Barbara, our translator Sergei, and I in Galina's small, spare office. With a good size wooden desk, cleanly painted walls and a wooden floor, the room was comfortable enough for one or two people, but clearly not designed for crowds. The men had hastily brought in extra metal chairs that were jammed next to each other tightly.

There was no artwork on the walls, no wallpaper. A lone plant sat on the windowsill, growing toward the sun, its stem and leaves rangy from the arctic winter. I noticed a black, old-fashioned telephone, the kind with a rotary dial, and I recognized it from the background of the fax picture I had received. Dima must have had his picture taken here, in this office, posed in front of the most concrete symbol of modern life in the orphanage.

"So," Galina said, "we will go over the medical records. I did send them, you know; I copied everything."

I told her that I had never seen anything but the picture. The medical records had gone astray somewhere or been way-laid, perhaps deliberately, perhaps not. In Russia, it was often hard to tell what had happened and why. I had begun to suspect that officials tried not to burden prospective parents with scary sounding medical information until after they had seen and fallen in love with their adorable little children.

Galina had a no-nonsense approach to everything. She was middle aged with short white hair combed back, neat and simple clothes and a cross that was conspicuously displayed on her chest every time I saw her. For a country that had gone for decades with religion deep in the shadows, religious symbols had sprouted forcefully, and appeared everywhere in a remarkably short time.

She told me Dima's story as she remembered it. "Dima came to us a year and a half ago," she said. "He had just had the casts off from his last surgery, and he was unsteady on his feet. That was understandable of course; he had never walked before. Remember his first day here, Tatiana? He seemed dazed, didn't he?"

She looked at Tatiana, who nodded, and chimed in, "At first we were worried about him, because he didn't talk. We thought perhaps he didn't understand things, that he was slow. Of course, that was before we knew him better," she added hastily. They talked mostly to each other, reminding each other of that time.

"At first, he hardly knew any words," said Galina.

"Just mostly medical terms," remembered Tatiana. "That's all he heard, being in the hospital all these years. He

33

knew the names of things like thermometers, stethoscopes, and blood pressure cuffs. But he didn't know words for everyday things, for animals, for toys. And he didn't use sentences; he just really had labels for things, medical things."

Later, when I thought about it, it would make perfect sense. He would not have had a chance to come in contact with any of those things in a Russian hospital in the 1980s. While other children were learning the words for "Mama," "Papa," "teddy bear," he was learning the words for "cast," "surgery," and "thermometer."

I tried to picture him, picture his life. I have a vivid image of him at about age three, small and pale, lying in a bed beneath stark white sheets, encased in a cast up to his waist, staring at the ceiling. In my mind's eye, he is lying there for hours in a darkened room, thinking amorphous thoughts, lacking sufficient language to put his ideas into words or to entertain himself with unspoken stories. Now, years later, I sometimes wonder if that's how he developed his extraordinary visual memory and unusually creative side.

Still, this was not at all what I'd expected to hear. The only hint I'd had about these early beginnings had been Allison's offhand comment that he'd "had hip dysplasia, but it's corrected now." The rest of this had been left unsaid. I hadn't considered the long years in a children's clinic, the lack of activities, the lack of attention. In Russia, the attitude toward handicapped children seemed to be one of resignation, of fatalism. Later, I read an article about the terrible conditions of children's homes designed for disabled children and began to understand the view that existed in Russia. One of the caretakers interviewed for that particular article said it was such a shame, that it almost broke your heart that "God has cursed these children, has fated them to spend their lives chained to a bed." She saw it not as cruelty on the part of the staff to treat the children so, but simply in the nature of things, an unavoidable way of handling a terrible problem.

Still, in Dima's life, I know that people had tried to make a difference. After all, hadn't he had difficult surgery to correct his problem, surgery that must have been expensive for the system to provide? And yet, when he was very young, the whole focus of their attention was to correct his problem, not to accommodate his emotional needs at the time.

"Why was he in the hospital so long?" I asked.

"He was in the hospital for all that surgery. How many times, Tatiana, three, four?" Galina asked. "For his legs - you know he had hip dysplasia? Of course they told you this?" Galina had leaned forward, concerned.

"They told me. But I assumed he had surgery one time. I guess I thought he was in a hospital for a few weeks. I really didn't think about it." My voice was a little higher than I would have liked it to be, and I was fighting for control. I was worried about the information I was getting.

"Three, at least," said Tatiana, with authority.

Galina broke in impatiently, "One, three, four, what's the difference? It's corrected now."

"But his lack of language?" I asked. This, and the emotional aspects of neglect, worried me the most.

"He did talk. Just not much." Galina looked at Tatiana. I could tell she didn't understand all this fuss about when he started speaking. Concern over his legs she understood better. It was a more definable problem. She leaned over to Tatiana, "Who did he have to speak to? No one. It was just him, lying on a bed in a hospital. The nurses, they are busy, how much talking can they do? You will see, when he has someone to talk to, he will talk."

I was nervous and disoriented in a strange country, a country that felt as though it were on the brink of revolution, and I was about to commit myself to a child I didn't know, a child who didn't appear to like me very well. I was unable to talk to my husband who was thousands of miles away, so I had many things to be anxious about. But I think in the back of my mind, the one thing I really worried about was adopting a child who would never be able to bond with me, who would be filled with anger and rage, who would be uncontrollable, who would disrupt our family irreconcilably. I knew the stories of children who, after being deprived of love, and shunted from one place to another, became unable to attach to anyone, used anger to distance themselves from people who reached out. I had worked professionally with such children and I knew that this behavior could completely disrupt families; I knew it would break my heart to try to parent such a child. I also was familiar with the work of Harry Harlow. Harry Harlow was a wildly controversial psychologist who pioneered studies on the role of maternal care and bonding between mother and infant primates.[9] At the time he was doing his initial work, there was a widespread assumption that children attach to their mothers only because the mothers provide food, and that holding or touching wasn't necessary. Harry Harlow also made some surprising observations when he needed to breed and raise monkeys quickly for a study involving surrogate mothers. In an effort to do that he had quickly and efficiently separated the monkeys from their mothers at birth. Unexpectedly, he discovered that instead of getting a ready supply of normal monkeys, he got monkeys who demonstrated bizarre behaviors. Baby monkeys who had been deprived of early nurturing often screamed suddenly, rocked themselves back and forth and lashed out randomly at their age mates. It would turn out that children who had experienced profound social deprivation, and had little or no opportunity for any normal social interactions with other, often displayed similar behaviors.[10]

Those considerations never entered Galina's or Tatiana's thinking, as far as I could tell. In Russia, there is a stigma about having a physically handicapping condition that transcends anything I understood. Children with physical handicaps are separated from the society, are often shunted off to institutions and hospitals. But the ideas of bonding and attachment problems apparently were foreign concepts to Russians at that time, or at least to the Russian people we met. Our views and expectations of families and children were so different, our ideas based on completely different sets of assumptions. Because we had so few assumptions in common, we had nothing to grab hold of in this discussion.

I had little concern about Dima's orthopedic problems; we would deal with them as we could. My real concern was about the possible impact of years of neglect. He had been described as having been left lying on a bed immobilized, staring at a ceiling, for months at time. He was so neglected that by age four and a half he had hardly developed any language. It seemed impossible that a child could emerge from such a situation emotionally intact and able to connect to a family. I knew that many people knowingly adopted children with emotional problems, and I could readily understand that. I had worked for years with children with emotional difficulties, and I found that they often touched my heart. But this was to be my first parenting experience, my first time connecting to someone as a mother, and it was the emotional connection for which I yearned. Galina and Tatiana were nonchalant.

"Orphanage delays," they said, with a dismissive wave of the hand. "All children raised in orphanages are a little behind; they need some time to catch up. A good home will do wonders."

I was beginning to feel panicky. No one but me seemed to understand. I tried to listen calmly and get as much information as possible.

Tatiana went on. "At first we really were worried about him. But after a few weeks, we began to feel very differently. He was unsteady on his feet at first, of course, but soon he started to walk better. We'd just gotten him out of the hospital and he had never walked before." She and Galina clucked about this.

Tatiana continued, "Dima showed interest immediately in all the things going on around him. He was interested in the lessons, he asked questions about animals and plants, he listened to the stories we read, and he paid close attention. But for the first month, his memory was not good."

She and Galina thought about this some more. "Let's see, he couldn't remember a sentence. From all the anesthesia, probably," Galina offered.

Tatiana agreed. "The anesthesia affected his memory."

This was a theory I had never heard before, but who knows? They told me that, after a month, his memory began to improve.

I had no theories about it then, but research would later emerge about many factors that can affect a child's memory. There is some indication that multiple anesthetic procedures especially may have effects on the developing brain. Stress is also a factor because children who experience extreme stress often have higher levels of the hormone cortisol, and that hormone appears to affect the development of the hippocampus, an area of the brain involved with memory.

"But there's something more about this child, something we all feel in here," Galina said as she clasped her hands over her heart. "Even though he has these problems, there is something about him, something special. He is so considerate of others, so kind, so caring. And he says things, things you wouldn't think he could possibly know or understand. He's like a little adult, like an old soul."

It was clear that Dima had a presence, an inner calm that affected the people around him. I could see in their faces, hear in their voices, that this child touched them, that they felt he was fated for a path in life other than the one he had been traveling.

I shifted my attention back to Tatiana who was still trying to describe Dima's early life with her in the children's home.

"Let's see," said Tatiana. "Oh yes, he had…" she and the translator grappled with some medical terms. The translator tried his best to explain what she was saying; it came out something like water on the brain, hydrocephaly, which is a very serious condition often resulting in brain damage and requiring surgical intervention. However, after we discussed this some more, it turned out that they were not talking about something so dire as hydrocephaly. They were talking about some diagnosis I think we don't have in this country. It is vague; it means something like a fluid imbalance in the brain, and many children have it, they assured us. "It makes them irritable, headachy, cranky; they must drink herbal teas for this," Tatiana explained. "It is really nothing, not so very important," she assured me.

My sister said, "Maybe, they have this thing, this diagnosis that explains cranky behavior. Sort of the way we have hyperactivity to explain problem behavior."

I glared at her. She often took pot shots at common psychological explanations that seemed obviously true to me.

Shaken by all this information, we asked if anyone else might help us to understand it better. They told me they had a developmental psychologist on staff who had assessed Dima quite recently, and they brought her in to our little room to answer my questions. I asked her if Dima would be able to have a normal childhood, go to a regular school. "Oh, yes," she assured me, "everything, all normal." I expressed concern over his early difficulties. "He will get over them," she said, "orphanage delays." She gave me a report she had written up. At the time I was grateful for the additional information, but it was only later, after I came to know Dima, that I would really appreciate the report and understand how startlingly accurate it was in most ways, how perfectly it described him.

It said, in part:

"Dima is a quiet, calm, balanced, kind, friendly, obedient and tender boy... He enjoys attention and caresses from adults. He is hurt by adult strict tone. When others have a nice attitude - he is obedient, hardworking and polite. He is punctual and frugal with his belongings. He is fond of knowledge and is interested in everything new around him. In everyday life he likes to draw, to look at and read books, listen to music, songs. He likes the programs about animals. He communicates well with other children, shares toys and books. He does not get himself in any conflicts. His favorite game is 'hospital' where he takes the role of a doctor. He adapts well in new settings. He gives a fair assessment of his own behavior.

He was admitted to the Child's Home at the age of five. His active and passive vocabulary was greatly reduced. He knew just a few common words, some of clothing items, pieces of furniture, dishes and toys... In his active speech he used 2-3 word phrases. From the first day he started to show an interest in classes and was very attentive and asked questions. But during lessons things had to be repeated to him several times and only after two months of studying Dima's memory began to improve."

When I look back at this document I am always amazed at how well it captured Dima's personality and how well it foretold the future. My son is hardworking, frugal, obedient. I was reminded of this document every time he followed me around the house, turning off the lights and discussing the high cost of electricity. He continued to balk at "adult strict tone." If I lost my temper and yelled at him, he would refuse to do anything. "My heart hurts," he would tell me. If I spoke politely to him, he would put his hand on my shoulder and say solemnly, "I understand how you feel about this, Mama."

Dima had such a tough start in life that I couldn't believe everything would just take care of itself. Orphanage delays are one thing, but Dima was deprived of normal interactions in his early life, and he experienced considerable amounts of physical pain. And yet, despite the fact that Dima had never lived in a family, he did not seem to have difficulties bonding to people; he was not disconnected from the world. He was warm and affectionate in appropriate ways. He did not have parents, but he had never given up on the dream. He wanted a family, he wanted a Mama.

As I pondered this, Galina took out some paperwork from her drawer. It looked strangely familiar. Then I realized it was my home study, an original and a translation. It had been part of my adoption packet that had been sent to her from the agency. She moved it into the center of the desk, where Tatiana could see it too.

"We have, of course, seen your home study, and we have just a few questions to ask you," she said.

CHAPTER 4

Myths and Stories

"All you need is love…" was the mantra of the social workers in the 1990s.

As Galina sat at her thick wooden desk with our home study open in front of her, Tatiana leaned over her shoulder so she could read the words more easily. Galina turned the pages slowly, browsing through my life, she and Tatiana murmuring from time to time. My history was laid out in front of all these strangers, strangers who were flipping casually through it, trying to determine if they should send a child in their care, a child they were completely responsible for, thousands of miles away, to my husband and me.

Galina shifted in her chair, and quietly poked Tatiana with her elbow now and then, as a particular paragraph caught her interest. I wondered what it was they really wanted to know, what information they hoped to wrest from this document in front of them. I realized their struggle was not much different from mine. Only a short time ago I had fingered Dima's faxed photograph, had watched the Syktyvkar videotape over and over, had called Allison frantically, all in the hopes of finding some clue as to who Dima was and what our life together would be like. By examining these pages in front of them, they hoped they could discover who I was, and what the future held for Dima.

They wanted to know, I'm sure, what kind of people we were. Why would we come all this way to adopt an unknown six-year-old child? How did we live? Who were we? They would find bits and pieces of answers to those questions in the pages on the desk, bland answers with the heart torn out. But those questions were irrelevant anyway, like my questions about Dima's life. The real question, the important one, the only one, was what kind of life would Dima and our family forge together. What would we create between us? It didn't really matter, after all, how wonderful or terrible the individual parts would be; it was how the pieces of our family would fit together that was important. And, of course, the answer to that question would remain a mystery no matter how many pages they turned.

But still, the home study was the only clue they had, although it couldn't have been much more help to them than my conversations with Allison about Dima had been to me. In the end, the decision would simply be an act of faith. They could make themselves believe that this was an informed decision, a cognitive decision, and they did. They read the information avidly; they soaked it up, like a plant drawing water through its roots.

As I watched them, I realized that I hardly remembered anymore what was in the home study; it was a blur to me. I thought back to what we had told our social worker about ourselves, what we thought was important for then-anonymous agencies to know. It seemed incongruous somehow that the things Frank and I discussed in the privacy of our kitchen with our affable social worker showed up here now, in front of these strangers - incongruous, but not unexpected, of course. After all, that was the point of a home study.

Our home study was not the traumatic event that many adoptive parents describe. Although I do remember that I cleaned the house, straightened up the stray papers that always accumulated raggedly on the tables, and put out a plate of fresh chocolate chip cookies, neither my husband nor I approached the visit from the social worker with any great trepidation.

In the movies, the social worker sent out to survey a prospective family is usually presented as either a stern or fussy woman, severely dressed, ready to cow the hapless would-be parents. But our social worker was nothing like any of the stereotypes. Kevin was the husband of a friend of ours, an easy-going, relaxed kind of guy. So when he showed up at the door in his Dockers and open shirt and offered us a big smile and a warm handshake, it was pretty much what we had expected.

When Kevin sat down at the table, he made it seem as though he were a long lost relative trying to learn something of the family history. I almost felt as though I should get out the big box I kept in my closet containing old black-and-white photos, the ones with the bits of black backing stuck to them, photos of grandma, grandpa, cousins, sisters, parents, aunts as well as photos of relatives only dimly remembered. And somehow, sitting around the kitchen table together, on that beautiful spring afternoon our home study evolved.

Although Frank and I both knew the home study would get sent to the adoption agency, we never pictured where it would end up, in the cramped little office in Syktyvkar, with earnest women scouring it for clues as to whether or not they were making the right decision on behalf of a favorite child. What would they learn about us as they turned the pages?

Kevin had written down that Frank grew up in Iowa, in a single-parent family, which was true. What they wouldn't know was that Frank's childhood had, in some ways, been as difficult as Dima's portended to be. Just as Dima's arrival in the children's home in Syktyvkar followed a path that was set long before he arrived in this world, a path we would never fully know, Frank's childhood was colored by events that took place long before he was born.

A family tragedy had happened decades ago in the Midwest that had set the stage for Frank's early life. Long before Frank was ever born, Frank's grandfather and grandmother had lived in a little house in Iola, Kansas with their five children. The house was set out in the flatlands, with quite a little space between it and its neighbors, an idyllic setting in which to raise a family. But fate often takes a hand, twists what we think is meant to be and throws us forcefully down a different path than the one we pictured. On an ordinary day, while Frank's grandmother was tending to a new baby, and the other children were playing by her side, the older children noticed that the pipe was loose on the gas line that went to the furnace. Breathlessly, they ran up to their father, Frank's grandfather, pulling on his shirt, blurting out something about a gas leak. He was busy tinkering under the car, and he wasn't paying attention. The kids were always finding something to stir their imaginations, to turn into an exciting scenario. He planned to check it out later that day, but in the midst of all his other chores, it slipped his mind. And by the next day, it was too late. The gas had leaked, something ignited it, and the house exploded. His wife and six-year-old daughter were killed. The story ran in the newspapers for weeks, and in the end, it changed the whole direction of the family. It was as though a tree were growing in the sunlight, in one direction, when suddenly a building was put up in front of it, casting a long shadow. Slowly, over time, it grew in a different direction altogether.

After the death of their mother and sister, nothing was the same. The four remaining children were left to struggle on. Mary, only four when this happened, grew up wild, unsupervised. She had no mother in her life; her father was increasingly absent. When she was barely seventeen, Mary married a local boy, divorced him shortly thereafter, and gave birth to Frank.

There is no way to know what Frank's life would have been like had the circumstances been different, just as there is no way to know what Dima's life would have been like had he been born into a different situation. Both were left to fend for themselves emotionally, to survive in rocky, unforgiving soil.

At seventeen, Mary was hardly ready for parenthood. She worked hard and partied harder and didn't have much time left over for anything else. When Frank was about two years old and Mary was nineteen, her friend told her that the army was recruiting women. She could join the army, go to exciting places, and meet exciting men. She signed up and, as an after-thought, asked her older sister to take care of Frank. Her sister was leading a stable life and was more than glad to have Frank, so he stayed with his Aunt Wilma for several years, until his mother came back from the army. Then, she took him back to live with her, and it would be the beginning of a childhood spent shuffling from one place to another. His mother's life drifted, and Frank drifted, too. They went wherever the work or the succession of husbands took Mary.

Frank told these things to Kevin, who condensed and summarized them. Galina and Tatiana would know that Frank grew up in the United States in the 1940s, and that he had lived with his mother. They would not know that Frank was in many ways like Dima, that he loved technical things but that he also loved ideas and words. And just like Dima, although he was neglected, shunted from place to place, and could have become bitter and angry, he reached out to people, developed a sense of humor. Although Frank acutely felt the hardship and stress of not having a stable family life, he became resourceful. He worked at odd jobs, even in grade school, and bought himself the schoolbooks he needed with the money he earned. At the time Frank went to school, each student was responsible for paying for the books he or she used, and the teachers or principal would call and remind families who were remiss in their payments. Frank's mother hated it when the principal called, bothering her for money for which she had better use. So Frank solved the problem himself when he was eight. He got a job shining shoes and running errands, and he told the principal to call him, that he'd pay for the books. From then on, he pretty much managed his childhood by himself.

As he told Kevin, he certainly had empathy for a child growing up without a family. The idea of saving a child from the kind of childhood he himself had had, appealed to him.

The family I grew up in was very different from that of my husband's. I grew up in the calm and quiet 1950s when the slogan was "I like Ike" and not much seemed to happen. My parents were Jewish, both professionals and rather quiet people, who rarely partied or drank. The best evening possible in my father's world consisted of sitting at home reading the *New York Times* and listening to the classical music station WQXR on the radio. Sometimes, *halvah*, crumb cake or bow tie cookies were available. My sister often said that one of my father's true talents lay in his ability to completely appreciate and enjoy the small things in life. "That man can make going to the bakery an exciting experience," she said. And it was true.

We told all this to Kevin, drew him into our lives for a moment, brought up feelings and memories long buried. Kevin listened empathetically, culled what he needed, and dutifully set it down, making the coherent "family background section" that Galina and Tatiana would read.

The central question of the home study focused on why we wanted to adopt and raise a child at all. And, of course, this was the question that Galina and Tatiana mulled over. Why would the crazy person in front of them want to do this?

This was a question I had grappled with for some time, and the answer was not readily obvious. Although we told Kevin all the usual things about loving and wanting children, even as we said them I understood how inadequate an explanation it was. I had never been one of those women who were passionate about babies and children, but I had always wanted a child. I had a complicated gynecological history, and I had discovered in my mid-thirties that a biological child might not be in my future. The idea of adoption had always appealed to me too.

The older I got, the more I wanted a child. I pictured taking my child sledding, walking, bicycling. I imagined family vacations, trips to the museum, and bedtime stories. It was not until after I got to be a parent that I realized that although I loved being a parent more than I could ever have imagined, it was for very different reasons. Sledding trips are cold, and the children whine; the museum is boring for children, and bicycling is better done with friends. But still, I would love being a parent. Being a parent is not the sum of day trips with small children. Even then, in some way I couldn't articulate, I understood being a parent is connectedness, being involved with another human being in a way different from any other; and, for a long time I had wanted that connection.

"But why Russia?" I could hear Tatiana and Galina murmur to each other. The truth was, we didn't exactly choose Russia, that part just happened serendipitously.

I thought back to our initial forays into the adoption world. The experience was a bit like Alice falling through the rabbit hole, finding a totally insane, nonsensical world. I had been a little fearful discussing some of our experiences even with Kevin because they were so strange, so out of context with the rest of our culture. But finally, after the home study section was completed, and we were, so to speak, off the record, we sat around comparing some of our experiences.

I originally had no idea of how to go about adopting a child at all, so I started with the phonebook. I looked up agencies and called a local one. The woman who answered was pleasant but no-nonsense. I told her my husband and I were interested in adopting a baby, and she told me that there were several ways to go about it. Then she asked me a few routine questions-what type of work we did, our education and so on. She also asked our ages. By then we were 38 and 48. I heard her sharp intake of breath when I told her that and I knew I was in trouble, but we made an appointment anyway.

When we met our adoption agency social worker, she explained that there were fifty couples ready to adopt every newborn. The world was a very different place than it had been when I was growing up in the 1950s and it was now difficult to adopt babies. In this country, in the 1990s, contraception was readily available and abortion was legal. Most women who had babies, single or married, decided to raise the babies themselves. Those babies for whom an adoption plan was made were in demand.

"Some people adopt children," we pointed out to the adoption counselor.

"Well, of course, that's true. I'm only telling you that at your ages it may not be possible for you to go through the public adoption agencies, at least for an infant. There are some other possibilities." She explained, "You can adopt privately. You've seen the ads in the newspapers, in the personal column. 'Loving couple wants to provide home for white healthy newborn.' You'd have to be aggressive, you know, really promote yourselves," she said. Especially at your ages, was implied. We somehow had never pictured ourselves aggressively pursuing a healthy white infant. We just wanted to raise a child who would love us and become part of our family.

Seeing the look on our faces, she continued. "You can contact an agency that places babies. But, unfortunately, our agency will only accept you to our program if both of you are under forty. Most other agencies have the same policy. However, there is another alternative," she said slowly, sizing us up. Her voice changed pitch for an instant, turning to a salesman like tone. "It's called the Blue Book. If you're flexible about the kind of child you can parent, this may be for you."

I knew what the Blue Book was, and I wasn't averse to looking in that direction.

My husband looked puzzled, though, and I put my hand on his knee, leaned toward him and said, "The government puts it out. It has descriptions and pictures of kids they're trying to find homes for, hard to place kids."

"You mean kids who aren't infants, or have some physical problems?" he asked. "That would work for us."

The social worker shifted in her chair and cleared her throat. "Well, sometimes it's true, we do get toddlers, or children with some physical problems. But usually, now usually," she stressed, "the children are older and have had," she paused again, "difficulties. Often the children in this book have emotional problems and have had several failed placements. We have many teenagers desperately needing families of their own."

We looked at each other. We had decided that we wanted, above all else, a child with whom we could connect, a child with minimal emotional problems. My husband leaned forward, "I don't think that's really what we have in mind. If we prefer adopting a younger child, a toddler perhaps, or a child no older than five or six years of age, with physical problems, how do we go about doing that?" The social worker sighed, "Well, in this country it isn't that easy. There are some children such as you described in the Blue Book, but you'd have to wait until you saw the child's description, and then apply. Usually there are scores of applications for the younger children."

"Surely there must be children, toddlers, who need homes," I said.

"Well, there are, but often they're not free to be adopted. The goal of the system is to re-unite children with their birth families, so children usually aren't free to be adopted from foster care until they are older."

This conversation took place in the early 1990s. Sometime after that, the process of adopting a child in this country who has been in foster care changed. The focus of social services shifted in the mid-1990s to finding permanency for children, as opposed to focusing solely on reuniting families. This caused a change in the laws and the procedures, but that's the way it was when we sat in that office discussing the Blue Book. We sympathized, we empathized, we understood the plight of the children in foster care, but it was not a challenge we wanted to take on at that time in our lives.

"But surely," we persisted, "there must be children in the world who need homes. We're not looking for those sought after, advertised, buzz worded, 'healthy white infants.'"

"There is another option," our social worker said, somewhat reluctantly. "Have you ever considered overseas adoption?"

Once the Pandora's Box of overseas adoption was opened, we fell into situations truly bizarre. Our first tentative peek into the world of foreign adoption was dizzying. Although the agency I spoke with didn't deal with overseas adoption, the social worker gave me the name of an agency that did, and I sent away for a pamphlet from them. In the booklet were the lists of programs they had, each country with its own. Each program offered children with different needs, and each had different parental requirements. It was sort of like looking for the first time at a menu from a Chinese restaurant where you had to pick from columns A, B, or C. If you adopted from Honduras for example, the children most likely would be sibling groups, and probably older. If you adopted from Korea you would probably get a healthy infant. Your own situation made you unsuitable for some programs. Our biggest but not our only problem was our age. Many, many programs didn't allow more than forty years between the oldest parent and the child to be adopted. Some programs, which allowed older parents, wouldn't allow adoption by parents if there were already other children in the family. They counted any children, even adult children born to one of the parents. A few didn't allow for divorce. We were all right in all the other categories that were sometimes factors. We had enough income, we owned a house, we were well educated, and we were married. We were a shoo-in in all those areas.

Finally, I braced myself to contact the agency that had sent us the brochure. I called the number, shifting from side to side in my chair, knowing this was a step in a scary direction.

The social worker told me that they facilitated adoptions from Central and South America, from India, and from many other places.

"Do you have a special country in mind, a particular type of child?" she asked. I didn't know how to answer that. Yes, I had a particular type of child in mind, a child in my mind's eye whom I had dreamed about for years, the one I pictured bicycle riding and skating with me, the one with whom I sipped hot chocolate on cold winter mornings. However, I was pretty sure that that wasn't what she wanted to hear, so I told her, no, I was simply open to ideas at this point. What a strange way to think about adoption.

Perhaps one of the most daunting experiences occurred when I actually had to sit down and fill out a form about child characteristics. The form was included in order to determine what problems a potential parent thought he or she could cope with. There was a list of child characteristics, each followed by the words "can accept," "can accept with difficulty," "cannot accept" and parents were to circle their response to each one. The listed traits gave one pause. There were seven pages of them, or about 140 listings of medical conditions, arranged by group. One category was physical and orthopedic problems, and under that was listed: limp, braces, missing limb, deformed hand, deformed arm, deformed leg, deformed face, missing ear, club foot. They were thorough if nothing else. It was a virtual catalogue of all the miseries in the world. It was bizarre, but it somehow changed my worldview forever. One of the hallmarks of parenthood is that no matter how it is achieved, through adoption or through childbirth, parents envision the future. They imagine their relationship with their child; they envision the child. Reading that form took me aback and made me realize that the world is filled with children with all sorts of problems one rarely even considered, and many of those children were struggling through, alone. It made me see parenthood in a different way. I became more attuned to the idea of appreciating whoever my child turned out to be, and being relieved just to keep him or her safe in the world. And as my dream shifted in some unfathomable way, I began to explore the options more fully.

We were told about an informational meeting that would be held in our town, at the home of a family who had just adopted a baby from India. We showed up at the appointed time and sat in the living room with about six other couples. They seemed to be in their late thirties and early forties, most of them middle class and nervous. At the front of the room stood a social worker, a plump authoritarian woman of about sixty years of age. I disliked her immediately, which is unusual for me. She began by telling us all, appropriately enough, about the programs available. At first, it sounded reasonable. But all of a sudden, to my horror, I heard her blithely explain that all the children from one particular program were premature or had medical problems and the mothers had had to surrender them because they couldn't afford the medical bills.

The social worker did not appear to be amenable to holding a discussion about this issue, or any other for that matter. In general she seemed to know that she was holding the trump card and played that to the hilt. She was in charge, and we were expected to comply with the rules, no questions asked.

My husband and I looked at each other. We walked out. We didn't want anything more to do with this process, and didn't discuss adoption at all for quite some time. But, somehow, I kept circling back to it, unable to let it go.

Sometime later, I contacted an agency in New York, a well-known, respected agency. The social worker told me that they had programs in El Salvador and Ecuador for which we would be eligible, and encouraged me to be flexible and at least consider children up to age five. I expressed concern about the ability of an older child to connect and bond to his or her family. I still remember her crisp tone as she told me, "We find that children of all ages bond well to their new families." It did not seem to me, that in the world of adoption agency social workers in 1992, people were interested in discussing the meager research then available on developmental issues or on emotional difficulties of bonding in older children. It was several years before the literature would come out about the extreme difficulties experienced by many of the Romanian children, in particular, and more attention would be paid to the issues of bonding in older children. The view of older child adoption swung from one end of the pendulum to the other in the years that followed, but in 1992, the theory purported by the social workers was "all you need is love." It seemed politically incorrect to even discuss the fact that children might have behavior problems. Later, reactive attachment disorder would make its way into the public consciousness, and every television series, it seemed, would have an episode about an older adopted child with violent and uncontrollable behaviors. Reactive attachment disorder appears in children who have not had an opportunity to bond to a caregiver early in life, and is marked by aggressive and sometimes dangerous behaviors.[11] The media would make it appear that older child adoption equaled reactive attachment disorder, but that was as far from the truth as "all you need is love."

In a few weeks the agency representative called. She had a child assignment from El Salvador for me. The boy was five years old and a full report on his health and background would be sent. The report was complete and well written, but the boy was still living with his parents. The agency told me his parents were abusive, and besides they couldn't afford to keep their children, and that he would be placed in an orphanage soon. I told them that this made me very uncomfortable. I couldn't adopt a child who already had a family.

"Well," said the agency social worker, as if I was being unreasonably squeamish, "if for some reason you're uncomfortable, we can wait until another child assignment comes through. Think it over."

I called back the social worker the next day. "I can't do this," I said. "It doesn't feel right to me."

"Okay," she said, in a voice that made me picture her shrugging, "I'll wait until we have a child already living in the local orphanage." She was accommodating, but spoke with me as though there were something odd about this request. From her point of view, this particular child would wind up in the orphanage anyway in a short while, and she would simply be finding a home for him a little later on.

It was then that I contacted World Child, an adoption agency that placed children internationally. Their offices were in Washington, D.C., but they were willing to accept us if we had a home study done by a licensed agency in our local area. They told us that they dealt with programs in Europe and that in these programs only the age of the younger parent was considered. The younger parent could be only 45 years older than the child to be adopted, and the age of the older parent was irrelevant. Since I was ten years younger than Frank, this worked out perfectly for us. They suggested a program in Hungary. Most of the children were toddlers ages two to five, and as orphanages go, this was a good one where the children were well taken care of and had good nutrition and toys. Among the requirements was that the prospective parents make one short trip there. When a child was assigned to the agency, the information they had would be sent to us to see if we felt that this was a good match. There were no implied threats about accepting the assigned child, no indications that anyone had been forced to give up any child. These were children who were already living in orphanages and needed a good home. We were excited and filled out the papers.

Three months later we discovered that the program had closed and the government was encouraging Hungarians to adopt the children. At that point, there were no other programs for which we were eligible (I still have a letter from World Child which reads, in part, "it is doubtful that any other country would accept a 53 year old father"). I remember calling my friend Anne, who was also trying to adopt and who was in a situation similar to mine, and we both sobbed over the phone at that. World Child, however, promised to keep our application and let us know if anything else opened for which we would be eligible. We held out little hope and the idea faded into the background. Only then, when we had pushed the idea of overseas adoption back to the far recesses of our minds, although we already had a partial complement of paper work sitting in the World Child office, did we get the phone call from Allison, the call that told us we were on top of her Russian List.

When we first decided on the option of overseas adoption, the specter of sitting in an office thousands of miles from home, trying to explain our lives and our reasons for wanting to adopt a six-year-old child, had not yet entered our minds. And yet, that is exactly the position in which I found myself, as I sat in the little office in the middle of an orphanage in Syktyvkar, thousands of miles from home.

Tatiana and Galina knew nothing about the kind of people we were, the choices we would make in life, the way we would treat our child. I could see them struggle for some type of understanding, but between the language barrier and the cultural differences, and the very short amount of time we had to get to know each other, it was impossible. It was an odd mix of knowledge that they had about us. In truth, they knew little of our feelings, our hearts.

No matter how little they felt they knew, they needed to make a decision. But, really, how much choice did they have? Few other options existed for Dima. Whether or not Galina and Tatiana understood why we wanted to adopt Dima, they apparently decided we were at least sincere. Finally, Galina closed the book to indicate she was finished.

"Congratulations," she said. I breathed a sigh of relief, although I knew from the beginning of the interview, there really could be no other outcome.

So with Galina's congratulations, I was about to become a mother. Dima would be my son, and the rest of the paperwork would be routine. How our relationship would unfold, however, would remain to be seen. In my mind's eye I could picture him sulking in the corner, and worry crept in. Yet, I knew, from the smile that flickered fleetingly across his face as we played, that there was another side of him.

My sister and I spent the next day and a half completing the rest of the paperwork, dragging ourselves from one office to the next. The first official we saw was a local judge, who interviewed us. We invited her to visit us in America and we were approved. The next morning, we waited for hours in an official-looking building until finally the head official stamped our papers and we presented him with a silk scarf. Everything that was needed for the final adoption was complete, and we returned exhausted to our hotel.

No sooner had we gotten into comfortable clothes than Sergei knocked on the door and excitedly told us that we were going someplace special and that we should dress up. It was to be a surprise, he said, nudging Alex, who was standing next to him. Instead of the grim, serious, efficient men we had grown used to, they looked like two schoolboys hiding a present.

My sister and I looked at each other and shrugged. By now, we were used to following directions without asking too many questions. We had brought a minimal number of clothes, but we did our best to dress presentably. We speculated about where we might be going, but it was useless; we didn't have a clue.

Alex and Sergei came back in a few minutes, still looking like children with a secret. They were obviously pleased with themselves. We followed them out to the street where they hitched a ride for us. This time we didn't even flinch as we got into a car driven by a total stranger. We were becoming acclimated to our new life. The car took us into the heart of downtown Syktyvkar and stopped in front of a large building that looked exactly like the surrounding buildings. Everywhere, the buildings from the communist era were stark, square, and white with no frivolous ornamentation. However, inside was a huge, elaborate reception hall used for weddings. Several weddings were actually in progress, complete with music, women in bridal attire and guests toasting each other. There was a surreal aspect to this. I was in a strange place where I knew no one. I had been going to official places and filling out official forms, and suddenly, there I was, in the middle of a wedding hall. A strange intimacy pervaded the situation; it felt as though all these people should be friends. As I was guided through the hall, my eyes met those of a young bride just returning to her wedding reception. She smiled at me, lifted her glass, and shrugged sheepishly, in a bit of a familiar gesture, a gesture to someone you have known for your whole life.

Apparently, Sergei, Alex, Galina and Tatiana had all conspired to give me a real adoption ceremony. They had invited several of the important people associated with the children's home, and ordered flowers, champagne and chocolate. This ceremony was to celebrate the creation of a family, but only my sister and I were here.

My recollection of the entire event is accessible to me only as a distorted, dreamlike memory. When I close my eyes and think of the moment when I swore to be Dima's mother and care for him the rest of my life, I see myself standing in the reception hall, with the sounds of weddings in the background. The judge was a fierce woman who, in my memory, is sitting way above me in an imposing throne-like structure. I am standing in an aisle much the way a bride would be, and holding a single red rose, which has been presented to me for this occasion by our translator, Alex. Despite a gruff exterior, Alex was apparently quite a romantic at heart.

The judge asked me questions in Russian, and someone translated. "Do you promise to care for Dima for the rest of your life, to love him, to cherish him?"

"I do, I do," I said. I told the judge emotionally that I would love Dima, that I had wanted a child for a long time, that I would do my very best. I would make sure that he had whatever he needed. My husband will love and care for him too, even though he cannot be here. I cried, and it seems to me that everyone around me cried.

I wanted them to know that even though I spoke no Russian and appeared in their country out of the blue to whisk away one of their children, I would be good to him. Ugly rumors had been circulating throughout the adoption world. Some individuals believed that people who come to foreign countries to adopt children do so for horrible purposes, for scientific experimentation, for body parts. I didn't mention any of this, of course, but that knowledge made me want to reassure all these people. For that moment they were all I had, they were like family, they were guests at the most important moment of my life, although I had met most of them only that day.

After the adoption ceremony, we went to a small private room for the reception. My sister was there, of course, and Tatiana and Galina, the judge, some other friends of Galina's who were involved in work in the children's home, Sergei and Alex. The only one conspicuously absent was Dima. Although I had promised to cherish and love him, he was not there to witness this; he was a child, and in Russia children are not part of the adult ceremonies. He had therefore, made no such commitments to me.

But there was no going back now. He was mine to love. And, surprisingly, I did. I know it is supposed to take time to form such a bond, but at that moment, I gave my heart to him and from then on, I felt as though he were a part of me. I am not sure I understand this myself, this intense love, for a child I barely knew, but that's the way it was for me. Perhaps it had to do in some way with the fact that I now defined him as mine. My child, my family, mine.

CHAPTER 5

A Week in Moscow

On that windy day in Moscow, when I left Dima's gloves on the plane, I lost his trust. I would have to travel a long, hard road to gain it back.

Finally, the morning arrived that we were to take Dima with us, away from the children's home. I was nervous, my palms sweaty, and I kept fingering the toys I'd brought for him, the things I hoped would keep him entertained. I was about to embark on the scariest part of this journey, the part that would set the tone for my relationship with Dima. I would be taking him from everything he knew. I hoped he would be excited about it, not frightened. Tatiana had promised that she would be there to say goodbye to Dima and to comfort him. We were scheduled to take an early plane from Syktyvkar to Moscow, and so we had to go to the orphanage in the quiet morning hours.

Dima later told me that one of the women woke him when it was still dark and told him to dress quietly and not wake the others. He didn't get a chance to say goodbye to

Nadia because she was still asleep, he said. Although he knew this was to be the last time he saw anyone here in the children's home, he was so excited about going on an airplane that he didn't think much about it. He was also excited about having brand new clothes. I had bought clothes for him in the States and had left a complete set for him. His other clothes would be kept here at the children's home for the next child who came to take his place, because, of course, there would be no shortage of children to fill the slot. He took off his Syktyvkar clothes, his plain pajamas, and began to metamorphose into an American Guy.

First, he put on his new Mickey Mouse underwear. He had never seen cartoons on underwear and wasn't quite sure what to make of this, but he did have an inkling of who Mickey was from the murals on the orphanage wall. Of course, the Mickey on his underwear did not wear work boots, but still, it was close enough. Next Dima put on his new jeans. For some reason, American jeans have become the symbol of status, of fashion, in other countries, and even in this remote part of the world, a six year old living in a children's home knew that this was really something classy. Fortunately, I had guessed right on the sizes of his new clothes, and even the new sneakers fit. Dima had never owned sneakers before and he could hardly believe his good fortune. But the *piece de resistance* was the red and black ski jacket. Later, he bragged about it to everyone who'd listen, bragged about its zippers, pockets, and bright colors. The last crowning jewel of Dima's new outfit was a fancy pair of gloves a friend of mine had managed to find for me. These were special, colorful Gore-Tex gloves, and Dima had never seen anything like them.

I had not gotten Dima a hat, so Tatiana, who worried about him in the cold, gave him the hat he had usually worn. It was a blue hand-knit hat with a string that tied under the chin. She explained that during the holiday season many people knit hats and mittens to give to the children's homes so the children would be warm. My husband and I have that hat still, folded up and stashed away on the top shelf of our bedroom closet, a reminder of Dima's other life.

When Dima finished dressing, Tatiana brought him down to the main room and they waited for us. He brought nothing else with him, except the book I had given him the day before. Only years later, when he complained that he could not fit everything he absolutely required for a five-day trip into his suitcase, did the import of this strike me.

Tatiana brought Dima over to us and hugged him goodbye. Unlike two days ago, when he had been sulking and morose, he was now cheerful and smiling. He played with the zippers on his jacket and showed Tatiana each of the hidden pockets and other wonders of his new clothes. He was clearly excited about the airplane ride, and made airplane noises and talked very fast to Tatiana. I stood back for a moment and just looked at him. He was adorable. A feeling of wanting to protect him, to keep him safe, washed over me. Just as I had been after the adoption ceremony, I was very conscious of the fact that he was now mine; mine to take care of and to love.

We all waved goodbye, and Sergei and Alex loaded us into the Army ambulance which would take us all to the airport. When we boarded the plane, I sat next to Dima. My sister, Sergei, and Alex sat several seats away. I smiled at Dima and took out a pack of crayons and paper, which I had brought for this purpose. Dima obliged me by drawing, and in a cooperative spirit, made objects on his paper. When I think back to that moment, I realize how my choice of toys reflected how little I knew of him, of his style, of his play, of his heart. Knowing what I know now, I would have stuffed my pockets with trucks, cars and Legos. And for good measure, I would have put in several sticks of gum.

Dima was charming on the plane, polite and happy enough to sit next to me. The flight was short, about an hour or so. We opened up little packages of peanuts, cans of Coke. He was quite cheerful during this flight. We snuggled close to each other, pointed out various aspects of the drawings to one another, looked out the windows at the clouds and sun. Then Dima gave me his brand new gloves to hold.

We landed at Moscow airport to find howling wind and blowing snow. We pulled up our collars, and Dima put out his hands for the gloves. I realized I had left them on the plane, which had just taken off again. I gestured to show I didn't have them anymore, and pointed to the plane. When Dima realized that I had lost his gloves, his whole expression changed. A scowl replaced his cheerful, sunny smile. Apparently, I was not a person to be entrusted with anything important. I was careless and irresponsible. This vision of me remained throughout the entire stay in Moscow and set the tone for our relationship.

In Moscow over the next few weeks, we collected documents everywhere we went, papers that needed to be kept with us for emigration. I kept them all in a brown accordion folder. Dima didn't understand exactly what they were, but he knew they were important and had something to do with going to America. He watched me like a hawk. Sometimes he insisted on carrying them himself. One time he and I were standing together, and I was holding the folder. The translator walked away from us, and Dima ran after him, liking the company of Russian-speaking people. Suddenly he wheeled around, ran back to me, abruptly took the document file out of my hands and ran back to the translator. The look on his face said, "I almost left those important papers with that careless woman. What was I thinking?"

Over the years, Dima has remained the same in this way, taking responsibility for details, although his attitude has softened somewhat. I think that now he knows I am a person to be trusted, a person who will keep her word, will stay with him through thick and thin. But though he knows that I will do the best I can, he isn't always sure that my best is good enough. He warns me to be careful on the ice. He worries about the condition of the boiler and he checks to make sure the roof isn't leaking. And, most of all, he worries about the people he cares about and, in his own way, tries to protect us from harm.

But on that windy day in Moscow, I lost Dima's trust, and I would have to travel a long, hard road to gain it back. All that week whenever we were outside, he jammed his hands in his pockets and looked mournfully at me, driving home the point that because of my carelessness his hands were cold. I did try to find new gloves, but it was hard in Russia. I managed to borrow a pair of mittens for him from the people we were staying with, but clearly it wasn't the same as having his own new Gore-Tex gloves.

So it was with a very displeased Dima that we returned to Zina's house. Babushka was there cooking lunch for us, and Zina was home, too. The smell of onions and potatoes simmering in the soup filled the air. We ate lunch together, Dima sitting quietly, his face immobile, now and then a tear rolling down his cheek. He didn't touch his food, and finally Zina suggested that he was probably tired, that a bath and a nap might help matters. The initial excitement of the day, the plane ride and the clothes, was wearing off and underneath was an exhausted, frightened, upset child.

I took Dima into the bathroom and filled the tub. He liked baths and was used to taking them at the children's home. The women bathed the children there, so he was comfortable with having me help.

He began to undress himself as I tested the water for him. He took off his shirt and there, around his neck, on a brown shoelace was a large gold cross. It was the last thing in the world I expected to see around my child's neck, and it startled me. In my family, no one wears religious symbols, believing in part that religion is a private, personal part of one's life. Our family often conducts itself like spies, giving people information on a need-to-know basis. Also, growing up in the shadow of the Holocaust, I learned it was best not to tell more than you had to. And, of course, since my background was not Christian, the cross on my child seemed especially out of context.

At that moment, I understood vividly that he'd had a life before me, a life of ideas and beliefs. He obviously treasured the cross and took it off his neck cautiously, dramatically, and laid it down ceremoniously on the bench. He pointed to it to make sure I saw he had something so important. It was really the only possession he had. Zina and I speculated about where he might have gotten that cross. I would not discover its origins until years later.

Once in the tub, he relaxed and, as he was getting out, even gave me a hug. I put him in my bed so he could take a nap. I was new at being a parent, and I expected him to lie down by himself and sleep. He was new at being a son and didn't know he could coerce a mother to snuggle down with him. He lay in bed silently.

As I was about to leave the room, I saw him look around mournfully, and two big tears rolled down his cheeks. He looked bereft, as though he'd finally grasped his situation: he would never see anyone he knew again. He'd left all that was familiar to him and was going off with two strange women he didn't know, to a life he could not yet imagine. I went over to the bed and put my hand on his cheek. He just stared through me. I couldn't even murmur words of comfort. We had no words in common.

Over the next few days, Dima's behavior vacillated wildly from polite and appropriate when we were out doing errands with our Russian translator, to absolutely out of control and hysterical when he was with me. He threw the doorstop at the wall; he had temper tantrums; and he took apart the cassette player I'd brought for him and unraveled all the music tapes. He purposefully and angrily slammed doors as hard and as often as he could. While I had expected difficult behavior and knew that it wasn't unusual for children in such stressful situations to behave this way, I wished I could do something to comfort him, wished I could win his affection. And, above all, I wished I wasn't so exhausted that I couldn't think straight.

I looked forward to going out with the translator to do paperwork tasks. These were almost the only times that Dima was calm. The first place we had to go was the American embassy that served as a center for all the Americans adopting children. When we had first arrived in Moscow, we had seen other adoptive couples during our orientation lecture concerning the papers that were needed. Now, as we finished our paperwork, we kept running into the same adoptive families over and over — at the embassy, at the American medical college, at the travel agencies. We compared notes about everything. We talked about the homes we were staying in, the translators we had, the agencies we were using, and the children we had adopted.

Most of the children were younger than Dima and seemed to range from about one year to four years of age. Russian law at that time stated that no children could be adopted internationally unless it was "for health reasons", which meant they all had some medical or emotional problems. Many of the problems were minor. Everyone was curious about everyone else's child and the tactful way of asking, "What problems does your child have?" turned out to be the famous question, "And why is your child being allowed out?"

Most parents I spoke with indicated that their children had medical problems such as crossed eyes, low birth weight, or generalized developmental delays. The description of a child's medical problem was often a tricky balancing act for orphanage authorities, especially when the child had a mild developmental delay rather than a specific, definable problem. The orphanage authorities wanted their children to be adopted, wanted to show the child in the best light possible, yet in order for a child to leave, he or she had to have a documented problem. What often happened was that the delay was explained in different ways to different people. To the prospective parents, the condition or delay was explained as what has been termed "orphanage delay," meaning that the child has no innate problem, but because of lack of stimulation and one - on - one care, the child was slightly delayed. The implication was that, given a loving home and good care, the child would come along. To the authorities in charge of approving the release of the child, the delay was explained in the paperwork as a significant developmental delay requiring special care and schooling. The truth usually lay somewhere in between, and for prospective parents, the situation was confusing.

One family we ran into several times was adopting two children. They already had two children at home that they had adopted as toddlers, they told us cheerily, but they wanted an infant. A baby had been located, but the orphanage where she lived said they had a six year old they were trying to find a home for and must be placed first. The six year old was a favorite at the home but had almost no prospects because of her age and the fact she had a shortened left arm. When a home was found for her, then the baby could go.

"What's one kid more?" the husband asked. "We love kids. So we are taking both."

I was amazed by his undaunted attitude, since I myself was terrified. It seemed somehow touching that the orphanage directors cared enough about finding the girl a home that they weren't above a little strong-arming to get her one - touching but a little scary, too. I think all the directors in the "baby homes" disliked sending children on to the homes for older children. These homes had reputations for being much worse than the places for young children, and the younger, frailer children were often at the mercy of the tougher, older ones.

As we sat in the waiting room at the American Medical College, where Dima was scheduled to have the mandatory medical evaluation, we met a family adopting four siblings. There was a handsome boy of about six years of age, a boy of about two and two twin girls of about four. I tried to talk to the mother to find out a little about the family, but she didn't have enough energy for small talk. She seemed so frazzled, seemed to be just barely coping.

There were some toys for the children to play with in the waiting room. Her son was trying unsuccessfully to engage Dima in play, the two-year-old was running wildly through the room, and the twins were playing, stealing glances at their new mother, and giggling evilly. I asked Sergei what the twins were saying. He shook his head,"Oh, nothing," he said.

"It must be really bad if he won't tell us!" my sister said, and we both laughed. Dima sat next to me, terrified, not talking to anyone. The only thing that seemed to cheer up Dima was that Sergei kept giving him change for the soda machine.

The exam itself was brief, but its effect on Dima seemed profound. Dima, my sister, Sergei and I were called into a room. A physician came in and gestured for Dima to get on the examining table. As soon as Dima got on the table, he became a different child. The child who had looked alert, albeit terrified, disappeared. His eyes became vacant; his body became limp and almost lifeless. My sister and I looked at each other in alarm. No one else even seemed to notice. My sister whispered to me, "This must be how he got through all those terrible times of surgery. He just disappears."

The physician looked at his throat, ears, listened to his heart. No blood work was done. Dima was already adopted and, as the man from the embassy assured us, once children are adopted they are never denied entrance into the United States. That was a big fear of all parents, since the medical evaluation took place after the final adoption. Any problem of getting the child into the U.S. at that point would leave a family in limbo. But we were assured it never happened. Since the evaluation did not include a blood workup, which would be the only valuable source of information for most parents, I couldn't figure out the point. I only knew it was terribly frightening for Dima, who I'm sure thought he was about to enter a hospital again, especially since the evaluation was located in a hospital building.

After the medical evaluation was over, we took all our paperwork back to the embassy. Dima watched every minute to make sure I didn't lose anything. When all our paperwork was finished we still had several days remaining before our flight home.

Although Dima was familiar with the Russian culture and language, his experiences with normal family activities were almost non-existent. After all, Zina's home was the first private home in which he'd ever been. He hadn't had opportunities to shop for groceries, to ride the metro, to eat interesting foods. We took him with us to get groceries and took him on some small excursions. He seemed absorbed with the details of everyday life, interested in everything he saw.

We shopped at the hard currency store, the store for foreigners, which accepted only dollars. The Russian stores in 1993 had almost nothing in them. People stood in line for hours for bread, sausage and milk. Fruit was virtually unavailable, and vegetables were scarce in the Russian stores, although both were plentiful in the hard currency stores. Nevertheless, exercising great ingenuity, the Russian people managed to obtain little delicacies. Most people lived in apartments in the city throughout much of the year but had small, simple summer *dachas* in the country. The *dachas* were described to us as huts, without electricity or running water. Families traveled to them by bus and train every weekend throughout the summer months and raised vegetables on small plots. What they grew, they brought back and used throughout the winter. Zina had even grown some coffee plants and brought them inside in big pots to her apartment. They looked beautiful, but she was still drinking tea because so far no coffee beans had appeared. In the ruble stores, people were able to get only basics-potatoes, macaroni, apples. An ingenious system of bartering for all sorts of goods had developed. For example, a woman who needed size five shoes would look in the paper for someone selling shoes. If she found a good deal but the wrong size, she would buy them, to obtain leverage in trading in another deal until she eventually found someone willing to trade her size. The details of daily living were exhausting. But here, in the dollar stores, anything and everything could be found. Zina's daughter, Katia, and Dima looked on in amazement. There were great bins of oranges and jars of coffee, which were almost impossible to find elsewhere. Prices were about the same as in the States, with a few things, like coffee, being more expensive. But for Russians these prices were beyond reach. I was told a Russian professor earned about forty dollars a month. A bag of oranges was about four dollars, a small jar of coffee was ten. So the Russians shopped in the ruble stores, and watched the foreigners walk out of the dollar stores with bags of groceries.

We brought back milk, fruit, meat and vegetables, everyone lugging a bag. Dima took as much as he could carry. It was clear from his effort and his cooperation that he felt responsible for helping. When we finally arrived at Zina's, after an exhausting combination of metro trips, Babushka had tea, sausage and crackers ready for us. She clucked and fussed over the fruits and vegetables, and said it was wonderful that we had fruit and milk for Dima. We sat down for tea and put the oranges on the table. Dima had never seen an orange before. We peeled it and held out a section. *"Apelsin"* Babushka cooed. Dima ate it and smiled. *"Apelsin,* Da!" he cooed back happily to Babushka. *Apelsin* was to be his favorite food for a long time, until in America he discovered candy bars and consolidated his love for Coca-Cola.

During the time we stayed with Zina and her family, they treated us with kindness and consideration. Despite our best efforts, I'm not sure our family treated them the same way. Six people, including a maniacally upset child, were all crammed into a small apartment. Zina slept on a foldout bed in the living room right next to the telephone, and I slept on her bed and my sister slept on Katia's bed. Dima slept on a foldout cot in an alcove and was unable to sleep through the night. My husband tried to call at reasonable hours but with the time difference of eight hours, it was difficult. We had to communicate information about travel arrangements and I felt as though Zina was constantly being awakened by calls for me.

Many of the calls involved our desperate efforts to reschedule our flight home. During this time, March 1993, the political upsets were of constant concern, and we wanted to leave as soon as possible. We were worried about a revolution. We also worried that any one of us would get sick and be unable to leave.

We had to fly from Moscow to Helsinki and Helsinki to JFK airport in New York. The problem was that though we could get the flight to Helsinki without trouble, and the following day we could fly out from Helsinki, we couldn't stay in Helsinki. Dima had only a Russian passport so we would not be allowed out of the airport. We would have to stay at the airport overnight with Dima. My sister and I looked at each other and looked at Dima, my exhausted, emotionally drained child who was flinging things around the room. "No, no," we told each other. However, if we wanted to find a flight home without a delay at Helsinki, we would have to wait a week. We weren't sure what to do. I called my own travel agent in Arizona rather than relying on the information I was getting at the Moscow office. He specialized in adoption travel and was used to these situations. He called back in forty minutes and told me, "If you can leave this morning, I can get you on a flight that leaves in two hours. Otherwise you have to wait until next week."

"I'll try," I said. "I need a ride to the airport. You can't just call a taxi here." Finding a cab in Moscow was nothing like arranging for one in New York. I would have to arrange everything with Sergei's help.

Once again, I called Sergei, he called Alex, and Alex called the chief adoption coordinator. A woman would be dispatched shortly to take us to the airport. The organization was amazing. There seemed to be nothing they couldn't do. We hurriedly packed our bags and Dima's bags, and kissed Babushka and Katia goodbye. The doorbell rang and a beautiful young woman in fashionable boots and jeans stood there. She spoke English and would be our translator. She said there was just enough time to get to the airport. Her husband was a fast driver, she assured us. This certainly proved to be true as we careened through the streets to the airport. We got to the airport about a half-hour before flight time. Howard, my travel agent, had told us to go to the FinnAir offices to pick up our tickets so we needed time to do that and to go through customs.

Everything seemed to be closed. We finally left a message with someone in one of the other ticket offices. We started through customs without our tickets, while our translator tried to get information. The custom lines were long. My sister and I had all sorts of souvenirs, pictures for people, stuff. We hoped it was all legal. We had to wait a long time for the people in front of us, but we were all waved through. Dima was amazingly cooperative. I kept looking at my watch. By now it was past boarding time, and I didn't hold out much hope of making the plane. Dima seemed to grasp the situation and kept looking anxiously at my watch, too, and trying to hurry me. I was carrying his packet of papers because I knew I would need them to get through immigration in New York. He insisted on taking them from me. He kept repeating, "America," pointing to the papers. As we successfully emerged from the other side of customs, my translator yelled, "Get on the plane. They are holding it for you. Run. Someone will come and bring you the tickets on the plane." So we did. Two grown women and one little boy who was holding tight to his package of immigration papers, running down the airport corridor must have been quite a sight.

The attendants politely and ceremoniously let us aboard and seated us. Sure enough, within a minute, a man came racing aboard, panting. "You are the Americans with the child?" he asked.

I nodded.

"Here are your tickets."

He got off the plane, and we took off for America.

CHAPTER 6

Making Up The Rules as We Go

Parenting a child who doesn't know you and who comes from an institutional setting requires different assumptions than parenting a child who has been with you from birth. Traumatized children tend to be much more easily triggered into crisis mode by everyday events and they are significantly less likely to be able to think their way to more rational solutions to the issues and problems that confront them.[12] Keeping stress low and managing the environment to be structured and predictable for them increases the chance for success in coping.

We'd done it. We had actually managed to get to Russia, negotiate the paperwork, adopt Dima, get him out of the country, and leave before a revolution. Our last task was to get him home. Our flight to Helsinki was relatively short, and Dima was enthralled enough about plane travel to keep from getting restless. I had been concerned about how I would communicate with Dima once we left Russia, but fortunately the man sitting next to us spoke both English and Russian and translated willingly.

At Helsinki, we had to change planes and board the jet for the nine-hour trip to America. Now, nine hours in a plane is a long time under the best of circumstances, but it is an eternity with a child with whom you cannot communicate.

We settled into our seats, Dima wedged next to the window, I in the middle, and my sister next to me. I looked around and noticed that most of the people on the plane seemed to be couples traveling with an infant or young child. The children seemed exceptionally energetic, definitely overwrought. It turned out that many of the people on this plane were families with newly adopted children. Howard, our travel agent, had managed to get us on what was essentially an "adoption flight." Apparently special planes were arranged for people involved in adoption procedures since their plans were more variable than those of other travelers. So, with us on our trip, were scores of new parents and their children. Most of the children were younger than Dima. Also, he was the only one, to my knowledge, carrying his own immigration packet, which he guarded fiercely.

In an effort to entertain Dima, I took out the photo album I had brought with me, an album containing pictures of the family. The first picture was of Frank and me standing in front of our house. "Papa," I said, pointing to Frank. Frank was smiling and looked himself, which is to say cheerful, jovial. He has gray hair-"silver" - he jokes. Dima studied him carefully and seemed a little confused.

"Grandpa," he said in Russian.

"Papa," I said.

"Papa," he repeated, looking a little disheartened.

I paged through to find something else that might interest him. I stopped at the picture of the family dog, Barker Parker. In the picture, Barker, a big brown dog of nondescript origins, is sitting on the deck, wearing a blue bandana around her neck. Dima was apparently thrilled by this and kept pointing to the bandana, laughing over and over. He seemed excited about the idea of having a dog. We flipped the page and found a picture of Franklin, my stepson. He was only nine, three years older than Dima, but he was huge by comparison. In the picture he is wearing a team sweatshirt and holding a baseball. Dima was fascinated by this photograph, possibly in awe of this boy who was, after all, already an American guy.

I put away the album and looked through my carry-on suitcase, trying to find other things to entertain him. All I had were the same old stand-bys of crayons and paper that clearly bored him now. I had hoped he would sleep on the plane, but it was clear that even though Dima was totally exhausted, he was not going to go to sleep. Instead he was heading for that manic, overwrought state that overtired children sometimes enter, where they become completely out of control, totally irrational. Most of the babies were sleeping by then, but one of the older children on the plane was running around, and Dima began to chase him. I made an effort to stop him, by holding on to him gently. He broke away from me, threw himself down on the floor, and tried to bite me, while kicking with his foot. Then he kicked the seat in front of him and whined. We were by now attracting lots of attention and his fuss continued despite the fact that I was talking to him in a soothing voice. However, luck was with me. The Russian - speaking man whom I had met on the first leg of our flight was on this plane, too, and was sitting in the row just in front of us. He heard the commotion and came over to the edge of our row of seats. He talked gently to Dima in Russian, and Dima immediately stopped kicking the chair and looked contrite.

The man leaned over my seat and talked with me. He told me that he had been born in Europe but had come to the U.S. to live when he was in his late teens, after the end of WWII. He currently lived in New York. He asked gently about Dima. How, he wondered, did I happen to have a child with me who did not speak my language? I told him the story, and he told me that he, too, had spent time in an orphanage as a child. His parents were killed in the war, he said. A shadow of sadness crossed his face. He said he could see that Dima was upset and bored, and that perhaps it would help if they sat together so Dima would have someone with whom to talk.

There was an empty window seat beside the man. Dima immediately calmed down on hearing Russian spoken, so I encouraged him to sit next to the man. Still clutching both his immigration papers and his photo album, Dima moved to the window seat. This gave me some time to calm down and try to regroup.

Dima sat next to the man for several hours. Finally the two of them returned, Dima looking very chipper and carrying a stack of magazines in addition to his other belongings. The man leaned over the seat and whispered, "He is a very interesting conversationalist," perhaps an unusual way to describe a six-year-old, but I was sure, nevertheless accurate. Apparently, Dima had told him, among other things, that he was going to his new home in Canada and proudly showed him the photo book. At that time, Dima wasn't sure about the relationship between Canada and the U.S., and I don't think he understood that they were mutually exclusive places - you couldn't live in both at the same time. He had apparently heard in Syktyvkar that children getting new homes went to Canada and he was somewhat confused. However, he'd also shown the man his album and had clearly identified Frank as his new Grandpa. "Grandpa, not Papa," he'd tell the man. He might have been confused about Canada, but he knew definitely that this man was Daddy. It's just that he had someone younger in mind to be his Papa, someone like Sergei, perhaps.

"He is a good boy," the man told me. "It will just take some time for you to get used to each other."

Once a calmer Dima was back again with me, the flight went faster, and soon we were ready to land in JFK airport, where Frank would be waiting for us.

The landing fascinated Dima. He saw the tall buildings come into view, saw the Hudson River, the cars. He even saw other planes in the sky. He was mesmerized. And then, the plane touched down, and everyone broke into cheers, and began clapping, as is a custom on long flights. Dima was excited. We walked out of the plane, me holding Dima's hand and an overnight bag, my sister carrying her overnight bag, and Dima holding his immigration papers, which he still refused to let out of his sight.

Dima and I had to go through the immigration line for non-citizens because he was still traveling on his Russian passport, while my sister whisked through the one for citizens. When we got up to the immigration booth, I showed the man my passport and Dima's. He smiled broadly at Dima, grasping the situation. The man explained to me that he needed to take the packet of immigration papers. The packet would be sent on to a main immigration office, be processed, and we would receive Dima's resident alien card in a few weeks. I looked down at Dima, still clutching the package. He looked at me uncertainly as I tried gently to take it from him.

"It's okay, buddy," I said. " We're here. We're in America." I pointed around us. "America."

He seemed to understand.

"Da, America!" he said, relinquishing the packet to me, smiling broadly.

As soon as Dima relinquished his immigration packet we were able to cross over to the other side of customs to Frank who hugged me and threw Dima up in the air. Frank carried him on his shoulders while Dima laughed hysterically. They were off to a good start. I myself was just thankful to be home. I wanted now to be at my own house with all its predictable comforts—my own bed, the family dog and my friends. But most of all, I wanted to sleep; I reeled from exhaustion. And somewhere in the back of my brain I had the uneasy feeling that nothing would be the same as it was before.

I didn't have much time to consider what would await me since we had to see my sister off to catch her plane back to Washington, D.C. As soon as she left, we hustled to find our car. A parking lot full of shiny new cars was something that could capture the heart of a six-year-old boy, especially this six-year-old boy. The car fascinated Dima. He walked around it, checking out all its features. Frank joined him and they both strutted around, pressing buttons, kicking the tires – male bonding, in progress. I know that most small boys like cars, but truly Dima seemed to have a bent for technical things beyond anything that would be predicted. My husband with his engineering background was similarly predisposed, so it was a great match.

We packed the trunk, with Dima instructing us on the correct and efficient placement of the bags, using hand motions and scowls. He not only was a dyed-in-the-wool techie, he was a definite control freak.

We all finally got into the car, and drove off. Dima sat quietly in the back. We had reached America, but we still had a four-hour car ride from the JFK airport to our home near Saratoga Springs, N.Y. Since there was no way for us to talk, Dima merely looked out the window and sang softly to himself in Russian. For some reason this touched me very much, and I thought of my grandmother, who, surrounded by people who didn't speak her language, often sang softly to herself in Yiddish. Dima's voice was sweet and gentle, and he sang on key, carrying the tune well. After a while he fell asleep, his head slumped against the window. Neither Dima nor I had slept in days, and we were both exhausted.

Although we were happy to be getting home, it turned out not to be an auspicious beginning. It was late when we arrived and dark outside. Dima was still asleep in the car, so Frank carried him into the house, trying to move quietly and not disturb him. But suddenly, without warning, there was barking, general commotion and something hurtling toward Frank almost knocking him over. It was Barker Parker, frantically running about, wagging her tail madly, thrilled to see us. Dima woke up suddenly and a look of absolute terror crossed his face. He freed himself from Frank's arms and jumped on the couch screaming "*Nyet Sobaka*" (no dog). I had shown him pictures of the dog in his little family album and he had seemed excited about having a dog, so this took me by surprise. Apparently, Dima had had minimal contact with dogs and what little contact he had was not especially positive. With all the other stress he was going through, this was just one thing too much. Little did I know that his fear of Barker and their problems adjusting to one another would be a major stumbling block, a source of aggravation for everybody. Sibling rivalry with the family pet? Who knew?

Finally, we were able to get some semblance of calm in the house as we put Barker downstairs and Frank coaxed Dima from his perch on the couch. Thank God it was night time and we could just go to bed and hopefully start over the next day. Dima fell asleep immediately. It would be the last time for years that he didn't require an elaborate bedtime ritual to fall asleep.

In the morning, I woke up groggily, in time to hear Frank whistling to himself as he dressed for work. Only three short weeks ago, I had a life with a routine of its own. I would get ready for work, have coffee, work all day, come home, and connect with friends. Things were abruptly different now. Yet I was thrilled. I could hardly wait to go see Dima.

I thought briefly of a story I had heard about a high school project designed to make adolescents more responsible and thoughtful about parenthood. Apparently, in this program, each student was given an egg that represented a baby, and he or she had to protect the egg, hold it, keep it with them twenty-four hours a day. The purpose was to impress upon them the degree of responsibility entailed in parenthood. I smiled to myself as I thought about it. It missed the mark because what they left out was the love. When you loved a child you were excited to do things that on the surface seemed deadly dull.

I peeked into Dima's room with anticipation. I watched with joy as he slept, breathing softly, snuggled in his covers. I kissed him on the cheek, waking him.

Abruptly, a scowl crossed his face, and I could see that he was momentarily confused, unsure of where he was. Then remembering, a look of terror crossed his face as he bolted out of bed. He ran over to his door and slammed it shut, yelling "*Nyet Sobaka, nyet Sobaka*" - no dog, no dog.

I hurried back to my room so I could capture the dog. I looked down to see our big, brown, weather-beaten dog, lying on the floor, thumping her tail. She had been so upset during the period of time that I was gone that she had barely touched her food for weeks. Now she was excited to have me back, even if I had come back home with a loud, scruffy, puppy without consulting her or the rest of the pack. I patted her head, and sighed. I took her gently by the collar and walked her to the basement steps. "Stay here, girl," I said, "I'll get you in a little while." The dog looked up at me and let out a little throaty moan. "I know, I'm sorry; I really am glad to see you." She thumped her tail again, which made me feel even worse.

I padded back to Dima's room where he was still barricaded behind the door. I opened it and said, spreading my hands out, "*Smateree, nyet sobaka*" using almost the only three Russian words I knew, in one sentence. (Look, no dog).

Dima came out of his room cautiously looking both ways to make sure the dog was not in view. Anyone careless enough to lose a brand new pair of gloves can't be trusted to keep a killer dog away from a child.

Dima followed me into the kitchen where he sat down politely and waited. He looked wordlessly at me and I looked back wordlessly at him. In my mind, I raced through ideas about what I could feed him. I knew he was used to potatoes, macaroni, and kasha, maybe. And we already had our *apelsin* success. I poured him a glass of orange juice and looked at him. I began making offers. I desperately searched for the Russian word for potato and excitedly remembered it. "*Khartoshka?*" I asked.

He shook his head.

"Cereal?" I said, trying enthusiastically to sell him on Rice Krispies, pouring them into a bowl.

He looked horrified as he peered down at the unrecognizable dried bits of colorless stuff in the bowl. He carefully moved the bowl away from himself, toward the center of the table.

"Macaroni? " I asked.

"Macaroni! *Da!*" he said. His whole face lit up. Macaroni was his favorite food, and one he got infrequently in Russia. Things were looking up from his point of view.

So there I was at 7:30 in the morning, in my bare feet and pajamas cooking macaroni while Dima sat at the table, politely with his hands folded, waiting. Normally, I would be showering and dressing for work, or, on a non-work day, lying snuggled in bed reading a newspaper or book, sipping coffee. My life had taken a quick change, too.

Frank came into the kitchen now, straightening his tie with one hand. His other hand was behind his back. He gave me a kiss on the cheek and peeked in the pot. He never knew me to cook anything of substance this early in the morning.

"Cooking macaroni, I see. A new addition to our breakfast menu?" he asked.

I glared at him and went on stirring the macaroni with a big wooden spoon. Frank went over to the table and stood close enough to get Dima's attention, to let him see that one hand was behind his back. Dima was easy. He immediately peeked around Frank and tried to see what was in his hand. Frank dragged out this ritual for several minutes, maneuvering his hand until finally he allowed Dima to peek at it a little at a time. Finally he opened his hand, and there, resting in his palm, was a silver colored matchbox car. It was one of those magical cars that sped forward by itself, after you rubbed the wheels on a hard surface. Dima had never seen anything so wonderful in his life, and ran up and hugged Frank out of sheer joy.

Frank threw Dima up in the air, and tickled him until I thought he would throw up, and then Frank left for work, leaving us on our own.

I spooned the macaroni into a large bowl and we companionably shared it. However, we had exhausted our communication resources and the day loomed ominously long before us.

I cast around for something to do. Hey, I'd watched "Leave It to Beaver" as a kid and I knew the one thing that always made kids feel comfy, that needed no words, was freshly baked cookies.

I went to work. I pulled out a cookie mix (I may have watched "Leave it to Beaver", but I'd been living as a working woman) and pulled a stool over to the counter for Dima to sit on. For the next half-hour or so, we cracked eggs, stirred ingredients, poured milk, and dropped spoons full of batter on cookie sheets.

We gleefully made criss-cross marks on the top of each cookie. He loved doing this, and carefully and meticulously made the pattern in each cookie, surveying his work with pride. And once the cookies were in the oven baking, he loved the smell of fresh baked goods that filled the air.

"*Panoffria*," he said, breathing deeply.

I don't think he'd ever experienced the smell of home-baked goods before. It was one of many of the small, but significant pleasures of living in a family, a real home, which he would experience. That June Cleaver knew what she was doing.

This however, was the good part. It lulled me into a false sense of security

The bad part was yet to come. I'm not sure what I envisioned doing with Dima, considering our lack of a means of verbal communication, but I think I had some vague idea of taking him to interesting child-friendly places like the park and museum. I had thought that now that I had time away from work, we could visit my friends, perhaps go hiking or canoeing. I looked forward to getting to know this child.

However, the week we had arrived home was the week after the huge March 15 blizzard of 1993, the one that had crippled the whole East Coast. Saratoga was still blanketed with wet, slushy snow making it impossible to go out and play. Once we'd finished breakfast, and baking there wasn't much to do.

And besides, Dima was in a different frame of mind than I was. He couldn't make his wants, even at the most basic level, understood. The food was unfamiliar, a killer dog roamed the house, and he would never see anyone he knew again. Sure, there were some benefits like oranges and cookies, interesting toys, and a big clean, quiet bed. But he wasn't even sure that this was his last stopping place. After all, he'd stayed in an apartment in Russia.

Much later, when Dima and I talked about that early time, he said, "You know, Mama, I didn't know what was going to happen. I didn't even know if this was my home, if I was going to stay here. I hoped I was because I liked it here and besides, I didn't want to have to get used to things all over again. I was very concerned."

By the middle of the first day, the stress was beginning to take its toll. Dima was beginning to look anxious, frazzled. As we both stared out the living room window at the view of the lake, it occurred to me that I could take Dima out for a ride in my minivan. Cars, after all, were a favorite of his.

The idea of going for a drive turned out to be the coup of the day. Dima's respect for me soared as we climbed in the van, he in the passenger seat, me in the driver's seat. I, a woman, could not only actually drive a car, I could drive a really big car. This was really something. It almost made up for the glove fiasco, I could tell. In Russia he had hardly ever ridden in a car and was usually transported in the army van. Most people didn't have access to cars, and few women drove. But here I was, his Mama, competently wheeling around in a big blue van. Pure admiration shone in his eyes as he watched me drive. The subject of the van would come up time and again in his conversation.

That first afternoon home, we took a ride around Saratoga Lake. I turned on the radio, and something on the news caught my attention. It was a report about international adoption and as it went on I was grateful that Dima couldn't understand English. It was full of scary reports of children with difficulties, stories that were just starting to emerge about attachment disorder. I looked at the child sitting next to me in the car, humming softly to himself. He looked back and smiled. I smiled too.

However, when we returned home, things took a sharp turn for the worse. When we had gotten home, after our drive, Dima looked up at the kitchen cabinet, put his arm on my shoulder and mouthed the word "suvachka." My memory has him almost whispering it, like an endearment. I had no idea of what it was all about. He persisted, obviously wanting something. Although he had started off sweetly, in moments he was almost shrieking, "Suvachka, suvachka." Finally he dragged me over to the kitchen cabinet, climbed on the counter and found the desired item-a package of gum he had noticed when I had been searching through the cabinets earlier. Obviously this was what he wanted.

Now, hindsight being what it is, I would immediately give it to him with a warm hug and make him glad to be there with me. But at the time, I was in my new mother mode, trying not to spoil him or give in to his every whim as everyone had warned me against doing. I shook my head, trying to explain he could have some later, after we'd eaten. He was inconsolable. Throwing himself down on the floor he proceeded to have a full-blown kicking, screaming fit.

Frank arrived home just in time to catch the tantrum, and to view my new parenting skills. At that point I was trying to coax Dima up off the floor with absolutely no luck, and was beginning to look a bit frazzled and hysterical myself.

Frank, however, was the picture of calmness and good cheer. He was carrying a big box in his arms, and he put it gently on the table as he kissed me hello.

"My, my, what have we here?" he said, smiling at Dima.

Dima, who had exhausted himself completely, was lying on the floor, head up against the cabinets. He just glared at Frank, warily.

However, Frank is the master of distraction with children and never ever worried about spoiling them. He went over to the box he had brought in and lifted out two tiny kittens, a gray one and a red one and cradled them in his arms.

Dima immediately got off the floor and came over to look at the kittens. He touched them and smiled. They were so soft. He cuddled the little gray one in his arms and it purred. This was something he could relate to. They didn't jump on him; they didn't look like they could bite or knock him over.

Frank showed Dima how to pet the gray kitten, and it purred some more and snuggled further against him. Dima was thrilled, and he and Frank sat for a considerable period of time playing with the kittens. The tantrum was gone, over, had left as suddenly as it had begun.

The kittens were a steady force in his life. We named the kittens Mac and Peridot, and over the next few months, Dima would drag poor Mac around everywhere. Mac had the best disposition of any kitten I have ever seen and he put up cheerfully with Dima. He snuggled in close to Dima, rolled on his belly, didn't complain that Dima carried him all over the house. Dima reveled in his soft luxurious fur.

The other kitten, Peridot, was more critical. It was good-natured, too, but it would not put up with everything that Mac would. Once, when Dima picked it up once too often, it scratched him. I heard Dima carrying him to the front door and dumping him on the front steps. He shook his finger at the cat and yelled angry Russian words, then, slammed the door shut. He still muttered *"plockat kashka"*. Bad cat.

Dima showed me his hand, which had a small red scratch on it. He told me something in Russian. I got a tube of antibiotic, a colorless, soothing cream, and spread it on the scratch.

Dima was delighted. I think the only antibiotics he was familiar with were things like iodine that sting. This stuff was soothing, and Dima needed anything soothing in his life right then. He took the tube from me, pointed to himself and announced "Dima's." In those first few months of adjustment, Dima kept the tube next to him almost all the time. He used it for touch ups on any little bumps or scratches. At night he set it down next to his bed. Then he would snuggle down into his blanket, ready for our elaborate bedtime ritual. Sleep often eluded Dima and our ritual was designed to coax him to sleep, to help him relax.

Every night Frank or I would read him a story and then the three of us would share a snack together. Then Frank would sit in the rocker and bring Dima into it hugging and rocking him gently. After Dima got sleepy, Frank put him into bed and turned on the radio and one of us would sit in the rocking chair until he fell asleep.

If we tried to leave before he was asleep, he would cry out piteously, "Don't go."

So we didn't.

CHAPTER 7

Dima Nyet Smile

Children who have not learned their first language with facility usually experience more difficulty with a second language. There are sensitive periods in language acquisition and children who have not had the normal opportunity to engage in language will be affected. Although children lose their initial language and replace it with the new language, there is a silent period in adoption during which the child is "between languages."[13] Communication, however, is more than verbal language alone.

O ver the next few months Dima's tantrums continued as I tried desperately to understand him. Every day for months, at about 4:00 p.m., Dima would have a temper tantrum. It didn't matter where we were, what I fed him, what we'd done. I think by that time of the day that he'd just had enough of not being able to talk to anyone, of being in a strange place, of being scared. He couldn't really speak English enough to make himself readily understood, and in the beginning, I learned about as much Russian as Dima learned

English. For about a month we were neck and neck, each having learned a couple of hundred words, perhaps. In addition to learning numerous isolated words, Dima also learned several phrases, but none that he used more frequently and fervently than the phrase "good boy" which he would say as he pointed to himself, smiling broadly at me. This followed anything he had just accomplished, no matter how terrible the deed.

Although I was frustrated by the language, I was not totally on my own. I had been given the name of a Russian family who lived in nearby Albany. They had emigrated from Russia a year or two before, taking only those things they could fit in their suitcases. I had spoken with the woman who spoke in broken English, but could understand enough to help translate. The family had come with two daughters, one a teenager and the other Dima's age. By some coincidence the younger daughter had the exact same birthday as Dima. The mother told me she would call Dima every night but as it turned out, she worked long hours at a variety of jobs, so it usually fell to the teenage daughter to talk with Dima. Rather than translate literally, as I had expected, she instead would talk to Dima and summarize for me his concerns, questions or impressions. She would then give him the gist of what I wanted to say, thereby leaving plenty of room for her own interpretation of events. Since she was at that stage of life where drama is all, her interpretations were frequently quite inventive and somewhat far from the original intent. What they lacked in accuracy, they certainly made up for in romance.

The first time I realized just how far her translations strayed was when she explained about the family van. Since Dima's first day at home, he had been fascinated by my van, impressed by my ability to drive it. His burning question to our translator, one he asked over and over again, was, "How come my mother drives such a big car, and my father drives such a small car?" He was obsessed with this question. I told her to let him know that we shared the cars equally but that I usually drove the big car because I had lots of stuff to cart around including him. She told him what she thought was a more interesting answer.

"Your father bought your mother a big, big car because he had a big, big love for her. If he had a small love only he would have bought her small car."

There was no use in my protesting. Until he learned English, I feared, Dima would get only our young interpreter's version of the world. What I didn't anticipate was that we would begin to develop connections with other Russian immigrants, all eager to help us.

It was during this time that I met Svetlana. She had heard about my situation from a friend and, having emigrated from Russia with her husband and her own son about four years earlier, was enthusiastic about helping.

She began calling Dima nightly and in a gentle way reassured him about everything. He would tell her about what he did during the day. According to her, he apparently was always very positive about the day's events and began almost every sentence with, "When my Mama took me here..." She told me he always emphasized his Mama and his family. But the sad note that kept coming up was my language deficiencies.

"Why doesn't my Mama speak Russian?" he would ask inconsolably. Svetlana would explain that he would learn English and that he must be patient. We still kept in touch with the family with the teenage daughter, but Svetlana had more time for Dima and more insight into dealing with him.

And although Dima and I did not have the words to express complex thoughts, and relied somewhat on translators, I quickly discovered that Dima was quite adept at making his feelings known despite his language limitations. He was clear in his opinions on most matters and although he may have been overwhelmed by this scary situation, this was no shrinking violet, no submissive, shy child.

For example, although Dima was impressed with my ability to drive a van, he was not impressed with the way I took care of it. As a matter of fact, he felt that the way I kept our van was slovenly. One day, as we were getting ready to go on one of our frequent excursions, Dima checked out the car to make sure it was ready. He was clearly outraged by what he saw. Seeing some towels left from a canoeing trip, extra shirts, juice boxes, an assortment of clothes, toys and snacks collected from a variety of day trips, he took me by the hand and brought me sternly over to the car. He then handed me the offending items, slowly, one by one. He handed me one odd swim flipper with a look of pure disgust, then handed me a towel, then one book after another. He then brushed his hands off and looked at me seriously.

"Dima *nyet* smile," he said. From there on, he let me know his displeasure large or small, with any of my actions, by the solemn look and the warning, "Dima *nyet* smile." He also frequently lectured anyone he caught committing an offense, pointing his finger in a scolding way for emphasis.

One afternoon I brought him over to a friend's house to play with some of the children. He still knew almost no English. One cheerful little boy of about six immediately tried to include Dima by playing ball with him. At one point the little boy accidentally threw the ball a little too hard and hit Dima in the face with it. Dima immediately put the ball down, and with one hand on his hip and the other pointing and shaking his finger, began to lecture the little boy in Russian. A quiet came over the room and my friend and I just watched, dumbstruck as Dima continued on and on, looking every bit like someone's Russian grandfather. As Dima concluded his lecture to the little boy, we all understood the final words, "Dima *nyet* smile!"

Dima also developed some effective strategies for negotiating for things he wanted. That spring, Dima was fascinated by bicycles. He had never had a bicycle, had never personally known anyone who had a bicycle, but he could hope. We had actually planned to get him one, but before we had a chance to do so, Dima took me by the hand and led me to the garage. There he gestured grandly to the three bicycles parked along the wall. He went over slowly to the first bicycle. He patted it gently and ran his hand down the seat. "Daddy bicycle," he said softly. He then looked at me to make sure he still had my attention. He moved to the next bicycle, also patting it gently and running his hand down its length. "Mama bicycle," he said, again looking at me. He then moved to the third bicycle, the one that belonged to his stepbrother, Franklin. "Franklin bicycle." He stepped back and sighed. He looked around the whole garage and shrugged his shoulders in an exaggerated manner. "Dima nyetta bicycle" he said sadly, shaking his head.

I ran over and hugged him. "Dima, Dima, you will have a bicycle." He wasn't quite sure what I was saying. "*Da*, Dima, *da* bicycle." I assured him.

"*Da?* Dima bicycle?" he asked, smiling. It was only a matter of days before a small green bicycle with training wheels showed up in the garage.

He also competently negotiated for a later bedtime. In April, about three or four weeks after Dima had arrived, the clocks were set ahead, making it light outside at his bedtime hour. One evening, after supper, he took me outside with him on the porch swing. He gestured expansively at the sky. "*Kraseva* (beautiful)," he said gently, awe in his voice, conveying the sense of wonder and beauty we both felt watching the sunset. Then he shifted to his real point, the reason he had brought me out there.

"*Nyet noche,*" he pointed out. Between the gestures and the glowing sky, it was clear that he was telling me that it was not yet night. Then he concluded his discussion. "Dima," he said pointing to himself meaningfully," *spat* (sleeps) *noche* (at night)." He sat back, his argument presented.

"Ah," I said, the light dawning on me. "You want to go to bed later at night!"

He nodded. "*Da.*"

"Okay," I said. I continued to be amazed that with almost no English, he was still able to "handle" me. And he was. I was no match for him. But I loved him, more and more each day.

Over the next few months, his personality would emerge slowly, and I would get glimpses of who he was. Frank and I would watch carefully, and smile in delight when we learned some new thing about our son.

Communication remained difficult despite Dima's gift for creative use of language and gestures. Despite all our best efforts, misconceptions and misunderstanding between Dima and us abounded. When I brought him to a home day care center near us, so he could play with some children, he clung to me desperately and refused to leave my side. He told the translator that night that I had brought him to visit an orphanage during the day. I desperately tried to figure out ways to introduce him to some children his own age, and although his reluctance to leave my side didn't bode well for his initial foray into school, I decided to bring him for a school visit anyway.

Dima had never been to school at all in Russia because he had left when he was still in the "babies" home where there was no school program. Had he stayed in Russia, he would have gone to the home for older children and attended school there. Usually each orphanage has its own school, designed as part of the institution. But of course, Dima's life veered off the predicted path abruptly when we adopted him and brought him home to New York.

There was a small alternative school in our town, one that sounded as though it might be a good place for Dima. I was encouraged when I spoke with the teacher, Joanne, who could only be described as enthusiastic and effusive. She was the American counterpart of Tatiana, the woman who was endlessly cheerful and warm with Dima in Russia. She suggested I bring Dima to the school early the next morning to take a look.

This was not quite as easy as it sounded. Dima was definitely not a morning person. When I tried to wake Dima a scowl crossed his face as soon as he awoke. I tickled him and said, "Where's Dima's smile?" This had become a morning ritual. I would spend five or ten minutes pretending to find the missing smile. "Is it here?" I would ask, looking under the pillow. "Is it here?" I would say peeking under the covers, until Dima could no longer resist and would begin laughing gleefully, uncontrollably. "Ah, there's Dima's smile!" I would say.

The rest of the routine consisted of cooking macaroni for Dima, laying out his clothes, and hurrying him along. He had only three speeds. Slow, slower, and stop.

The morning I was to take him to school boded well because it involved a trip in the van, which was always greeted with excitement. We drove the twenty minutes or so to school, Dima bouncing up and down in his seat.

"*Bystryj, bystryj,*" he shouted, (faster, faster). If I passed another car he yelled with glee, "*perigenales*" as we whipped by, and would look at me with pure admiration. I must admit, although I am generally a somewhat tentative and slow driver, I picked up the pace considerably that spring, encouraged by Dima's enthusiasm for speed and for passing other cars.

Joanne greeted me warmly at the door and reached gently for Dima's hand, to lead him over to a group of children. He shied away and predictably, clung to me. Joanne was unfazed. "Why don't you plan on staying with him, we love to have parents in the classroom," she said, without missing a beat. "We play music while the children put their things away and then we have circle time. The two of you can sit together and watch."

Dima remained by my side, sitting as close as possible without actually being on my lap. This wasn't a traditional school setting, and there appeared to be room for individual idiosyncrasies. The school had begun only three years ago, and had only a total of thirty children in it. We both watched as the children, who ranged in age from about five to eight years of age, sang songs, did their calendar reports and discussed the plans for the day.

By playtime, Joanne was able to encourage Dima to move several feet away from me, although he kept an eye on me, and motioned to me that I wasn't to go far. I obeyed and sat on a chair close by to the play mat. Joanne brought him over to a group of boys who were playing with wooden blocks and toy cars. Dima stood back for a moment to survey the building materials. He then joined the group, quietly at first. He began stacking blocks carefully, working by himself until he had finished a rather complicated structure. Not only was this an elaborate building with turrets on the top, but the bottom was designed to be open. As he finished, several of the other boys came over to look at it and admire it. Dima smiled graciously, then, showed them the truly miraculous feature of his building. The bottom opening was just the right size to drive their toy cars into and was, in fact, a garage. The other children began, by use of gestures, to ask permission to use the garage, and were soon asking Dima to design other structures for them.

"Well," said Joanne, leaning over to me, "getting along with others doesn't seem to be a problem."

"No, it doesn't," I said, thinking back to that early report in Russia indicating that he worked and played well with others.

Joanne had suggested that Dima and I stay for lunch that first day and I had brought along a little brown bag lunch. The two teachers and the thirty or so children in the school all ate together and after they finished, the children were all responsible for throwing away their own garbage.

Dima took out his food from his brown bag. He had milk, a peanut butter sandwich, and an orange. I took the orange and began to peel it for Dima while he worked on the sandwich and milk. When I finished, I put the peels in a little pile, and handed Dima the orange sections, which he ate, *apelsin* still being one of his favorite new foods. When it came time for him to throw away the little pile of garbage, he carefully took the milk carton and sandwich wrapping and went up to the garbage pail, leaving the mound of orange peels on the table. He then returned, pointed to me, indicating I should take the peels up. I gestured to the other children who were throwing away their own garbage. He shook his head, showing that he had no intention of throwing away the orange peels. I saw the teachers now looking our way, little smiles involuntarily curling up the corners of their mouths, watching to see who would win.

Finally Dima took the little pile of orange peels and very solemnly slid them across the table to my side. I slid them back. He looked at me sharply, pushed them over again and dusted his hands off.

By this point Joanne was laughing out loud. She came over and whispered in my ear, "I think since you peeled the orange, he thinks it's your responsibility to throw the peels out." That's exactly what he did think.

"I peeled it for him; he ate it. That makes it his responsibility," I protested. Joanne gave me the kindergarten-teacher-look.

"I don't think you'll have much success explaining that to a six year old, especially one who doesn't speak English," she said quietly.

I threw out the orange peel to avoid a further scene and an argument I could see I wasn't going to win. The tone of our relationship was already set.

After lunch, Dima went up to Joanne and smiled at her. "Bye, bye, Joanne," he said, and began tugging on my arm, pulling me toward the door. The noisy classroom was okay, but enough was enough. He was ready to go back to our cozy world together.

"I think he's had enough for one day," Joanne said. "Bring him back tomorrow."

And to Dima she said, "Bye, bye, pumpkin. I can't wait to see you."

He smiled back. It was love. And he was making his first connections to people outside the family in his new life. From then on, Dima began attending his little school three mornings a week until the end of June.

It was during this time, when we still had minimal ability to communicate with one another, that Dima came up to me one night, and I was alarmed to realize, as I put my hand on his forehead, that he was burning with fever.

"What's wrong?" I asked him futilely. "Do you hurt anywhere else?"

He looked blankly at me.

"*Boula?*" I asked, my only Russian word for ache, but one that I think translated roughly as "boo-boo" or bruise. What I had really been aiming for was a word that would suggest something much more dire, like a burst appendix or a strep throat.

He looked skeptically at me, and shook his head. No *boula.*

I sighed and looked at the clock. It was about eight o'clock on a Sunday night. In my experience with illness, no one ever gets sick at any time but Sunday night, when it is impossible to see a physician without going to an emergency room.

I led him to his bedroom, and he was so ill that he gratefully crawled into bed. I took his temperature and found that he was running a fever of 104 degrees. I put a cold cloth on his head and gave him a children's Tylenol. I looked at the clock, hoping it would give me some answers. I really didn't want to take him to the emergency room. I knew he was terrified of hospitals, and I wouldn't be able to explain what was going on. He continued to run a fever, accompanied by chills throughout the evening. I finally called Svetlana at about eleven o'clock at night.

"Find out what's wrong, if you can" I begged her. "I can't even tell if he has pain in one area, or if he just feels sick. Oh God, I hope he doesn't have appendicitis."

She talked to Dima and told me that he didn't have any pain anywhere, he just felt hot, felt terrible. Despite my having given him Tylenol and keeping a wet cloth on him, his temperature was still 104. She and I planned that I would keep him at home all night if his temperature didn't go any higher. Otherwise, I would bring him to the emergency room and call her, no matter what time of night it was, and she would meet us at the hospital so that she could interpret for us and explain to Dima what was happening. I was terrified, too, that he might be allergic to any medications he would need. There was a cryptic note in his medical records that care should be taken with his immunizations because of allergies, but there was no hint as to what these allergies might be.

Dima lay in his bed looking miserable and scared. I wondered if I had done a disservice to him, bringing him to a strange place with people he couldn't talk to, thinking we could do better for him. The arrogance of it, I thought.

I sat next to him throughout the night and held his hand, and put fresh cool washcloths on his head. He slept on and off, and with the Tylenol in him, the fever hovered between103.5 and 104. When the Tylenol began to wear off, he would start getting warmer and warmer, and would wake up. As soon as he awoke, I gave him water to drink and more Tylenol. I sat there willing for this to pass, willing for him to make it through the night without going above 104, the magic number.

As I sat there in the dark of his room, watching him sleep, wringing out his washcloth, I thought about my mother and I remembered how she had cared for me when I had been in the hospital as a child. My mother had died about three years before I adopted Dima and so she had never seen him, but I thought often about her when I first had Dima home.

During this night, I thought about my own experiences with hospitals as a child. I had had surgery when I was six years old, and had spent some scary weeks in the hospital. I had had a dermoid cyst on my ovary, an unusual occurrence for a child of six. I would later develop some other gynecological problems and there was some speculation by my doctors that I'd been exposed in utero to DES.

I was assigned a bed in the children's ward in Beth Israel Hospital, and I would, in those days before managed care, stay for three weeks. My bed was next to a white tile wall, and I have a strong memory of waking up the first morning there, trying to figure out where I was, staring hard at the tile. I panicked while I struggled to figure it out. The room was lined with beds and I remember vividly that my bed had sides on it with slats that could be raised up at night. It looked rather like a crib, or a cage, depending on your point of view. I hated having the sides put up at night, and remember later on pleading with the nurses to just leave them down, but to no avail. I assume now, of course, that the side bars were put up so children couldn't fall out of bed or wander, but they made me feel like a baby, and also made me feel trapped.

I didn't know it that night, but Dima also spent time in such a bed when he was in the children's clinic in Russia and passionately hated having those bars brought up and being closed in. He would tell me later on about his hospital experiences, and would say, mirroring my own thoughts, "I was in a cage. Like an animal at the zoo."

It always struck me as strange that Dima and I had such a similar experience, such a similar reaction, separated by about 35 years and thousands of miles. Sometimes it seemed to me that Dima's and my medical problems were in some cosmic way related to each other. They brought us together. Throughout my childhood, I often overheard my mother tell others in the family, "Well, the doctor says she should still be able to have children, but if she can't, she can always adopt." The idea of adoption became close to my heart, something familiar, and I always thought it would be a part of my life, although I had assumed I would have biological children as well.

Still, if I had not had the medical problems I had, I probably would not have sought to adopt a child right then, and if Dima had not had the medical problems he did, he would not have been allowed to leave Russia in 1993.

But that night, as I sat next to Dima, I thought about the three operations he had endured already, operations with no mother there to soothe and reassure him. He had no one to hold his hand, no one to rearrange his blankets when he was immobile, no one to put moist towels on his lips, only busy nurses, overworked and harried to provide minimum care, maybe a kind word now and then.

I remembered how different my experience was. The night before my surgery I was not allowed to have water and my lips were parched. My mother sat with me, wetting my lips with a cloth, stroking my forehead. And the night after my surgery, she stayed with me all night, sleeping in an armchair next to my bed. In those days, parents were not permitted to stay in their child's room during the night, but the nurses didn't have the heart to throw her out.

I had experienced, as Dima had, not only the fear and pain of surgery, the tremendous sense of a loss of control that comes with knowing you have no say about what will happen to your body. But unlike Dima, I had my mother near me, and I trusted her judgment and that made an enormous difference.

But still, being in a hospital had an impact. Death and disease were ever-present and I took account of them in a way I never had before. I was especially concerned about my own mortality. I can remember one sweet, gray-haired lady who came into the children's ward nightly and read us stories. One time she asked each of us why we were in the hospital. When she got to me, I told her I had a cyst, and then added, "But I don't know what that is and I hope I'm not going to die."

She was clearly unprepared for that answer and simply moved on quickly to the next child, who, it seemed to me, gave her a more satisfactory answer since that child knew what was wrong with her, and didn't throw in any unnerving comments. It was clear to me, following that interchange that it made people uncomfortable to hear questions about dying and I didn't bring it up anymore with adults.

Dima had spent years in a children's clinic surrounded by illness, estranged from any permanent caregivers. I wondered now how he had stood it, how he had come through all of it as unscarred as he did. I thought about that all night, sitting there.

Dima slept through most of my thoughts, but once and a while he would wake up from his troubled sleep, reach for my hand and turn over again. In the morning his temperature began to go down and stayed at 101 that day and then went to normal. I brought him to our pediatrician, but we never did find out what was wrong. But the emotional effects of that night went deep. I felt a gratitude to Svetlana, a comfort in knowing she was there that was overpowering. And it deepened my relationship with Dima. He had been scared too, and the effects of having a mother's hand to hold were not lost on him. Even now he mentions it. Every once in awhile he'll say, "Remember when I first got here and I was so sick and you held my hand all night?"

And once I asked him what he thought of that night. "I was so sick," he said, "so hot. But you know, it was really nice to have a mother."

CHAPTER 8

Adoption Mysteries

Parenting an adopted child brings to the fore the idea that what is important has to do with understanding and discovering your child, rather than helping him or her realize your expectations.

*M*y connection to Dima became so encompassing that my former life was cast off and rolled into a ball, shoved in a corner. My focus had shifted, and, surprisingly, during this time I never thought back to that other life. Friends would often call to see if I wanted to have lunch out or take a walk, or just get together, but in those first few months, there never seemed to be time. And besides, there was nothing I wanted to do more than spend time with Dima.

Perhaps Dima's excitement and appreciation for having a mother fueled my maternal instincts, or perhaps it's just natural to be engrossed with your new child, whether that child is a newborn or a six year old. It was exciting to catch glimpses of who this child might be, and I craned my neck, as it were, to get any little view of who he would become. In that way, an adopted child is somewhat more of a mystery than a biological child. With a biological child, at least you have some clues as to what to expect, or think you do, at any rate. I come from a family of lawyers, doctors, social workers, teachers, and writers. Our quirks tended toward depression, inattentiveness. I have a sense of who these people in my family are and some of the traits a biological child might have.

But Dima was a mystery to me and it was thrilling to see some of the unexpected qualities that he had. As his personality emerged, I could catch glimpses of his quirky mix of abilities and difficulties. From the very beginning, Dima had a fascination with machinery, and an uncanny understanding of the physical world. One evening when I put him in his little makeshift turtle bathtub (we had only showers up to that point), he sat contentedly splashing and playing with his little plastic boats. Finally, he tried to anchor one of the boats, but much to his increasing frustration, it kept tipping over. He gerry-rigged various contraptions, most involving sponges, soap, or scrubbies with string, and empty bottles, in an effort to get the boats to stay anchored and upright. These devices became increasingly complicated, but to no avail. Finally he sighed and said, "Not stable!" The hair on the back of my neck went up. He didn't know many words for common things, he certainly didn't know the alphabet, and yet he knew this word, this concept, before he could put together a complete sentence.

It was sometime soon after that we went to visit a friend of ours, taking Dima with us. He still spoke very little English and I can see him then, wearing a tee shirt that stuck to his ribs, showing off his skinny arms, and looking particularly young and frail. Our friend was enchanted by him, and in an effort to amuse him, brought out something special - a beautiful hand-carved airplane.

Frank and I admired it, noticing the colors and the detailed carving. Dima bent forward to look at it. He smiled with pleasure and reached out for the airplane, turning it over, looking at it from different angles. He pointed to various parts, then, suddenly, his eyebrows drew together, and a shadow crossed his face. He looked puzzled. He started gesturing, pointing at a little silver valve, a valve almost hidden on the underside of the plane. Neither my husband nor I had even noticed it, but it clearly had Dima's attention. He kept gesturing to it, pointing, shifting from foot to foot with excitement. My friend looked at us, puzzled, wondering what all the fuss was about.

I sighed. "I think he wants to know what the valve is for, what it does," I said.

"It's pretty complex to explain, but basically it's an intake valve that sucks in cold air to cool the engine and blows out hot air," he said.

Dima had only a few key words in English at this time, and we knew only a few Russian words. I told our friend the Russian words for hot and cold, and he used these in his demonstration, gesticulating wildly to fill in all the information between the words hot and cold. Dima listened intently. All of a sudden his whole face lit up. He started pointing at the valve excitedly, talking fast in Russian. His gestures showed he had grasped much of what our friend explained. He smiled, satisfied that he understood what the valve did, and handed the plane back.

The three adults just looked at each other wordlessly. The whole interchange had an eerie quality about it. Finally, my husband looked at me and whispered, "Maybe he's been here before?"

"I don't know, do you think he's an aircraft designer who got reincarnated?" I whispered back.

This thought would come to me again many times in later years as he built increasingly complex aircraft carriers, planes and missile bases all over our home, using whatever materials he could find. He was definitely driven to build, driven to understand technical ideas, to figure out how things worked. And yet there were hints, even early on, that some things, basic things, would not come easily to him. Despite his facility with mechanical things, letter sounds, words, language syntax seemed to be beyond his grasp. This child was definitely an enigma. He was complex; he was interesting to talk to and to try to understand. And from the very beginning, even with only rudimentary language skills, he had a wry adult sense of humor that gradually became more evident as he gained the language skills to express himself. He was even able to extend his humor to his always strained relationship with Barker. One day he came to me and whispered gently in my ear, "Barker plays the *pianino* (piano)." "Barker plays the *pianino*?" I asked, wondering where this was going. "Da, Barker plays the *pianino*," he said, nodding his head solemnly. Then he looked at me with a little smile creeping up in the corners of his mouth. "But Barker has no *ruchies* (hands)! he said, rolling over and over on the floor at his own joke about the fingerless, handless dog sitting at the piano, belting out tunes!

He carried his joke one step further. The next morning he woke up very early. I asked him why he had gotten up so early. He looked at me and sighed. "Barker plays the *pianino*. Too loud!" he said, covering his ears with his hands and making a wincing face. Then he shook his head and walked away. I laughed, too.

And I also knew that the phrase, "It's too loud" had a special place in Dima's heart. It was really the first phrase he had learned that had given him power over his environment. Before that he knew words like coat, jacket, car, hot, cold. But this was different. It was a phrase that let him control his life with words. I can remember vividly the day he learned it. He walked over to the radio, smiled at me and, putting his hands over his ears, said, "It's too loud!" and gently turned it down. He then gleefully ran through the house turning up the volume of the radios, the televisions, softly shouting, "It's too loud!" and then turning them down again. He especially loved this because loudness was always an issue for him. He hated loud noises. But now he was using this favorite phrase as the punch line for his joke.

I stood there looking after him, shaking my head. How did a kid who hardly knew any English, who never had anyone to joke with him, get such a sophisticated sense of humor? But with this, as in many things, I found that for some inexplicable reason, he just came that way.

But even though he hated noise, and even if he imagined Barker playing the piano too loudly, Dima did have a special place in his heart for music, and we were very fortunate that a thoughtful friend managed to get us a tape of Russian children's songs. This was not an easy thing to find in 1993. The first time we put on the tape, Frank, Dima, and I listened attentively. Many of the songs were familiar to me, including the Russian version of the "The Wheels on the Bus," which I'd heard often enough in English to want to scream. However, Dima fell in love with this tape. It was the only thing he owned which provided familiar words and sounds to him. For a long time he listened to it every single night, fell asleep to its music, and then kept it under his pillow during the day so no one would take it.

In addition to the Russian tape, we had one other powerful tool to help Dima fall asleep at night during those first months. Aunt Barbara had given him a beautiful panda puppet from China that became a part of our bedtime ritual.

"Put Panda on, put Panda on," Dima would beg every night before he went to bed, and I would take out our puppet. He had soft black and white fur, ears that stood up like a real panda's, sewn-on eyes and a red velvet lining. And what a personality Panda had. He was rambunctious, quick to take offense and get angry, quick to forgive. He was very vain about his beautiful black and white fur and his soft ears. And Panda, too, was not with his first panda family and had to get used to being in a new country with a new family. He'd come from China, even further away than Russia. So Panda understood Dima and Dima appreciated him dearly.

Yes, Panda became an important part of our life. Dima and I would have our snack, listen to music and talk to Panda. If Dima's favorite song on the tape, a hauntingly beautiful lullaby came on, Dima would say "Shh. Listen, Panda. Isn't it beautiful?" Panda cocked his head and listened, snuggling down next to Dima. They both listened raptly, in love with this tape.

Sometimes, when music wasn't enough to put Dima and Panda to bed, we would all watch old movies. One time Dima, Panda and I watched the old Disney cartoon version of "Peter

Pan." I had loved it as a child and Dima loved it, too. He made ticking sounds every time the crocodile chased poor Captain Hook around, and clapped earnestly for Tinker Bell. But when the scene appeared where Wendy came to the lost boys and they sang, "Now We Have a Mother," he became absolutely glued to the television set. He sat forward, his jaw slightly open. He turned to me excitedly, when the song was finished, and said, putting his hand on my sleeve, "You may not know it, Mama, but that's a really important thing. It makes a big difference when you have a mother."

My eyes filled with tears, and I kissed him.

And often, Dima told me how glad he was we picked him, what a good decision we'd made. "I think you made a really good choice, mom," he'd say. "I think you're a really good mother for me." He pointed out to Panda how well we got along, and the fact that we had the same color hair and other concrete details of our sameness.

During the first few months here, this theme would come up for Dima, over and over again. One evening as I was tucking Dima and Panda in, I noticed a cut on Dima's arm and asked about it. He explained that he had fallen from a swing, and I remarked, absentmindedly, that he was lucky he hadn't gotten hurt when he'd fallen.

"I'm lucky in lots of ways," he said. "I'm lucky I have a Mama and a Papa. I'm serious, Mama, you may not know this, but there are lots of children in the world that don't have Mama and Papa. And it's very important," he advised me.

One night, Dima had a little talk with me. I remember the moment exactly. He was sitting in his huge double bed, wearing his green Aladdin pajamas, his comforter pulled up around him, his hair still wet from his bath. He had just put in his Russian music tape, and before he turned it on, he took my hand and looked directly at me, for emphasis. "Dima take three airplanes," he said, holding up three fingers to emphasize his point. "Dima *doma* (home), no more airplanes. Dima stay here, right? Someone say 'Dima go,' "Dima say, '*Nyet*, Dima *doma*.' Dima stay right here, okay?"

"Dima *doma*, absolutely," I said hugging him to me.

I was delighted with the tight connections our little family was just beginning to make. Reports had begun filtering through about children adopted at an older age, especially children from Eastern European orphanages, who were having extreme difficulties, who were not adjusting. I would hear a news report about parents wanting to disrupt an adoption, or parents beside themselves because their new child showed angry, violent, bizarre behaviors, and I would look at Dima playing quietly with his blocks and breathe a sigh of relief. Sure he had tantrums, but mostly they were borne out of the frustration of not being able to make himself understood. I hoped that adjustment problems would not surface later, but somehow I felt that since he was already doing well, that if I could just keep things stable, without too many sudden changes, he would be fine.

But life is often unpredictable, and ours changed in a significant way not too long after Dima came home. My stepson, Franklin, who was living with his mother and grandmother, had visited sporadically at first and did not have a huge impact on Dima's life in the beginning. He came for visits once in a while, staying for the afternoon. Since we were hampered by language and had difficulty explaining even the most basic things to Dima, it was well beyond us to convey the subtleties of life. Therefore, Dima was unclear as to Franklin's role in the family, but he was happy enough to have another child with whom to play and Franklin was cooperative and good company.

However, when Franklin began visiting more regularly and began staying with us during every weekend, it brought a whole new complexity of relationships to be negotiated. It was a situation that I was somewhat unprepared to deal with, since I had expected that our relationship with him would continue as it had been.

Once Franklin began staying for the weekends, Dima became distraught. He had been developing his cozy spot in the family, with unlimited attention from a doting mother and father. It was a real luxury for him, a coveted spot in the sun. And now, some other child seemed to think he could just horn in on all this. Dima was enraged.

"Make him go home," Dima would say, clearly.

We tried to explain that this was Franklin's family too. "Daddy is his Daddy, too," we told an incredulous Dima.

"Well, he can't have my Daddy. Let him get his own Daddy," Dima replied. You could tell he was thinking, "*The sheer nerve of some people, thinking they could just take a perfectly good Daddy away from you.*"

At first, the fighting was constant on the weekends that Franklin was with us. One morning, I awoke to hear yelling and scuffling. I found the children in the family room, shoving each other. On cross-examination, I determined that Franklin had woken up early, turned on the television set and was about to watch cartoons when Dima came in, ready to watch also. Each had resolutely determined to sit in the best chair in the room, the recliner. Franklin, being bigger, stronger, older, faster, got there first and Dima was left to sit on the edge of the recliner, pushing at him.

I separated them and then left the room to make some coffee and start breakfast. Big mistake. I had no sooner left the room, than Dima came running toward me shrieking, sobbing. "He kicked me, he kicked me, he kicked me," he yelled. Despite his still somewhat limited English he seemed to be able to describe brotherly brutality clearly and succinctly.

I went into the room. "Okay, Franklin, what happened?" I asked, using a tone of voice that even I didn't like.

"It was his fault," Franklin said, uncomfortably, wriggling in his chair. "I was sitting on the recliner. I got there first," he said looking up at me plaintively. "He tried to make me get off and he couldn't so he sat on the leg rest. You told us never to sit there, that it would break the chair. So I kicked him to make him get off. "

"You're not to kick him for any reason. Ever. Do you understand?" I asked.

Franklin nodded quietly. Dima smiled self-righteously at him, poking his head out from behind me. This was not bringing out the best in anyone. I sighed, and worry settled in with me.

Dima was clearly becoming overwrought and anxious, edging out of control. That morning, after the scuffle, he opened the refrigerator door, looking for something, and began gesturing wildly. When I couldn't understand him, he completely lost it. He wound up down on the floor screaming "*sok, sok!*" which I later understood to be juice. The intensity of his anguish, his rage exceeded my wildest expectations and unnerved me completely.

As I stood in the kitchen, watching him, Franklin came in and stood in back of me, near the corner of room, watching everything. Finally he said quietly, as though thinking things through, "You know, you should punish him when he does that."

I probably should have smiled to myself that Franklin was so mature and self – contained, but I couldn't appreciate that yet. It was difficult that, in addition to worrying about Dima spinning out of control, I also had the discomfort of being judged by a nine year old. I told Franklin that Dima was frustrated, that we needed to be patient.

Franklin shrugged, "I don't know, I think my grandmother would make him stand in the corner or go to his room," he said. But he watched, and took things in, and began to understand my point of view, bit by bit.

I went over to where Dima was sprawled on the floor and tried to figure out what he was yelling about. I looked at a list of common words Svetlana had given me and figured out that *sok* was juice. I was talking softly to Dima and offering him various liquids from the refrigerator and he was beginning to calm down. I poured some juice for him, and, as his sobbing decreased, led him into the living room to sit down.

Franklin had come in seconds ago and had sat down on the nearest chair, the only child-sized chair in the room, the one that I had bought especially for Dima. It was Dima's favorite chair and this had the predictable effect of upsetting him further.

"It's my chair" he screamed, "it's my chair, make him give it back."

"Dima, just let him sit in there for a few minutes, he's not hurting the chair. Besides it's here for everyone to share." I said, reasonably.

"It's mine, it's mine. You gave it to me, it's mine," Dima sobbed, hysterically.

I hoped that Franklin would let me off the hook by moving to another chair, but he resolutely sat his ground, and showed no inclination at all to move. He was nine years old, after all, and wasn't doing anything that would usually be considered out of line. He looked on quietly as Dima hurled himself back on the floor, sobbing.

My husband was still asleep. I woke him. "This can't go on," I said. "I need help. I can't manage them both. They are both on the edge."

"Oh, come on, honey. What am I supposed to do? They're just kids, give it some time. Besides, Franklin's only here for two days at a time."

In order to try to calm things down, I took Dima with me to do some shopping I had to get done. Not a good idea. He was already distraught from the arguments that morning, and, once upset, he did not easily calm down. In hindsight, I realize the mall was probably one of the worst places I could have brought him, with all the noise, excitement, and general stimulation revving him up further.

We stopped first at K-mart where I planned to pick up a few things before heading for the grocery. The store was inexplicably jammed that morning, with crowds pushing us to and fro. I got a cart and began to go down the aisles, throwing in several items as I went. All of a sudden Dima saw a huge toy truck and pointed to it.

"Dima's," he said.

"No," I said distractedly, pulling him along with me, just wanting to finish up in this noisy crowded place and leave.

"Da, Dima's," he said, refusing to budge. Since I couldn't move him, and was determined not to give in, and was feeling relatively hurried and hassled, I repeated "No," firmly, then tried to cajole him into moving. It was a lost cause. He was already so worked up from the morning, and generally in such a tense mood, nothing would dissuade him. He also felt, I later learned, that I was being totally unfair. If I got to put things in the cart, he should be able to choose things, too.

In any event, at this point he hurled himself on the floor in a full-blown tantrum. I realized there was no point any longer of even thinking of shopping. I put the cart off to the side, and went over to try to pick him up and remove him from the store, much as you would a toddler. However, although he was skinny and small for his age, he was strong, and at six years old, was not easy to pick up and carry. I tried my best. However, he tried harder.

He grabbed my hoop earrings and pulled as hard as he could, as I howled in pain. People were clearly beginning to stop in their tracks and watch us. I took out my earrings, put them away and tried again to pick him up. I made the mistake of putting my hand too close to his mouth and he stretched his neck, reached out with his mouth, and bit me. I persevered, lifted him up and brought him out to the car.

I waited until he stopped kicking the dashboard, and drove straight home. The car radio came on, and I remember hearing the news headlines flash, one about a Russian adoption gone wrong. It was an overwhelming moment for me. Despite my earlobes hurting, and my hand throbbing where he had managed to sink his teeth in, I still felt this overwhelming sense of connection to him, this need to protect him. I loved him. I'd had moments of worry before, doubts about whether I was handling things right, doubts about whether things would work out okay for us all, but this moment was different. Before, even through my doubts, I remained optimistic. Now, I was scared.

By the time we got back home, Dima was clearly chastened. I ordered him to go to his room, and I went to the sink and ran cold water over my bite mark. I told my husband what had happened and he went into Dima's room and gave him a stern lecture on not biting anyone. Ever.

Franklin sat quietly in the living room recliner, trying to stay out of the way.

Dima remained in his room most of the afternoon, quietly playing with his toy trucks. When we told him he could leave his room, I noticed his eyes were red and he looked distraught with grief. Later that afternoon, he came up to me, shifting from foot to foot and solemnly asked if parents could exchange a bad child for a good one.

"You mean, like give back a child because they've done something wrong?" I asked, startled.

Dima nodded.

"Of course not," I said.

He was so relieved he began sobbing. "See, I told you so, Franklin," he muttered as he passed Franklin.

I gave Franklin a sharp look, but he just shrugged as if to say, "I have no idea where he came up with that."

By the end of the weekend I was drained, done, exhausted. But strangely, Dima, who had argued with Franklin all weekend, who had been frantic and out of control, was even more upset when he left. I watched the two of them as Franklin got into the car. Dima, who had wanted Franklin out of his way, it had seemed, threw himself down on the ground tears streaming from his cheeks at the thought of Franklin leaving. I wasn't sure what to think.

"Thank God it's only on weekends," I said to Frank.

CHAPTER 9

The Panda Puppet Stories

Puppets can offer understanding and a way to communicate fears, hopes and dreams. They are especially useful for children who have experienced traumatic or stressful situations since personal stories can be recalled at a distance through the puppet's story. Puppets can also serve as non-judgmental listeners.

*A*s Dima plunged back into stress, it seemed as though we spent more and more time with our beloved Panda puppet. Panda became Dima's companion, his sounding board. And Dima's conversations with Panda were, for me, a window into his past life, into his view of the world. Dima discussed with Panda his views on family, his hospital experiences, and his current life.

As we snuggled into bed, Dima, and Panda looked over our photograph albums. Dima had no photographs of himself prior to joining our family; there was no sense of continuity. When we got our first photographs back from the photo shop, I showed them to him. He was absolutely ecstatic.

"Dima's pictures," he said, taping some of them up on his wall and putting others in the little photo album I'd given him on the plane. He would point out the pictures to Panda. "See it, Panda, see Dima." And he would pore over the albums. "Look, here's Dima and his family." Sometimes he would pat Panda and say, "Don't feel bad, Panda. I know you lost your first family, but you're part of our family now. I'll show you our family, okay?" He told Panda that he knew he was sad that he didn't have his real Panda family, his first family, but that we loved him very much and would take care of him. Dima also told Panda how he, Dima, had had another mother who loved him very much but that she had died so he needed another family

Dima often talked about his first family and told me stories about them. He had never known this family, but he had imagined them. I didn't have much information about his family, but I had no reason to believe they had died. I tried to be honest, but to let him have his own interpretation. He was adamant that his family had died, and I let it stay that way, although later he would ask more questions and we would discuss other possibilities.

We spent night after night looking at our pictures, Dima, Panda and I, snuggled down under Dima's blanket. One night, instead of looking at our latest photos, I took down the family albums, albums that spanned the years before Dima arrived. As I showed Dima and Panda the pictures, Dima pointed out that there was no Dima.

"Where's Dima?" he kept asking as he looked through all the photographs.

"You're not here yet!" I explained.

"Why is Franklin in there?" Dima asked as a picture of his new brother, taken when he was younger, showed up.

"Franklin is there because he's in our family even though he doesn't live here."

Dima was totally exasperated by this explanation. He, Dima, was in our family precisely because he did live here. How did Franklin get to be in the family without living here? It was no use, but finally, without any satisfactory explanation, we moved on.

But, Dima was still upset. "Put Dima in, put Dima in," he insisted.

"Okay, okay, Buddy," I said, and turned to a fresh page where I could add pictures of Dima into our official-looking family album. And it got to be a routine. Every few weeks we would add more pictures of Dima: Dima with the cat, Dima riding a little truck, and, always, Dima smiling widely.

"Dima's family," he would say with satisfaction. Sometimes he would see pictures of babies, either in our album, or in other children's homes, and he would point out sadly, that no baby pictures of Dima existed in our album. Dima's recorded life starts at about age five and a half, with the first faxed picture I was sent of him.

One day, as he was looking at the pictures of smiling babies in our album, he said, "Mama, that baby is so happy. I wish I had been a happy baby."

"Weren't you?" I asked cautiously.

He looked at me scornfully. "Well, what do you think? When I was a baby I was in a cast. And these three older boys teased me all the time," he said, with disgust in his voice. "The nurse came in and yelled at them, 'You leave that baby alone.' But they wouldn't," he said, a tear rolling down his cheek. "No, I don't think I was very happy. You know I didn't get to come home until I was six. Before that there were mean big boys. I was not in my family."

"See it, Panda, I was in a hospital for a very long time," he said stroking Panda's fur. "I had to have surgery," he said, sighing. "I know you understand all about that, Panda."

Panda showed an ability to understand a remarkable range of problems, including physical ones, because Panda had some physical problems himself. Panda had no leg problems (he was a puppet; he had no legs), but he had an eye that kept coming off and required frequent surgery. At those times, Dima and I would talk quietly to Panda about his need to get the eye fixed, and the fact that we would be there for him when he woke up. Dima and I would darken the room; Dima would give Panda an anesthetic, and I would surgically repair his eye with needle and thread. Dima would allow him to rest that day and night, comforting him continuously, telling him how brave he was, how well he was doing, assuring Panda he would have a full recovery. Dima told me that Panda was a little self-conscious about that eye, especially since he was always so proud of his beautiful soft fur.

Dima was to tell Panda many things that he remembered of his own life in the hospital. As he explained it, he couldn't walk until the last surgery, so the women held him up by his collar with one hand, held another child by the collar in the other hand, and walked with them both. After the last surgery he was in a wheelchair for a long time. He explained that he couldn't run like the other children, but he could catch with his hands, and the children did play catch with him, as he sat in his wheelchair.

But he was so angry during that time. The last time he had had surgery, he told the doctors he didn't want to have any more surgery. But still, the next day he woke up in pain, in a cast, despite the fact that he hadn't given anyone permission to do that. He felt so angry, he told me, he wanted to punch those doctors, but he couldn't. Instead, Dima had refused to talk for almost a month to the doctors or with anyone else for that matter. This was the first time he talked about this to anyone. He patted Panda and told him his surgery was necessary, and he hoped that Panda wouldn't be so angry.

Once he told Panda, "You know, I stayed in a hospital for a long time." My curiosity got the best of me, and I interrupted him and Panda to ask him what he remembered of that time.

"Did anyone come in to play with you? You know, here, lots of times volunteers come in and talk to the children, play with them," I suggested, hopefully.

He gave me one of his "*What planet are you from?*" looks. "No. They treated me just like an adult. You know, they just left me alone on my bed. They didn't do anything with me until I went to Syktyvkar."

Those were his exact words, etched in my mind. They didn't do anything with me. And it's true. Galina and Tatiana had told me that they knew that before they got him, he just lay on his bed, in his cast, busy nurses bustling around. But once he got to the children's home, he listened to stories read by the stern women in sturdy shoes, and drew pictures, played with big wooden trucks, and went to physical therapy where he rode a tricycle, walked with a book balanced on his head and played catch with huge balls. But by then, he was four and a half.

Sometimes Dima told Panda other stories as he fell asleep; often Dima told about the women in the orphanage. There were different ones all the time, he explained, and some of the women were mean. Often these stories focused on the hardships Dima endured in Russia, the lack of varied food, the rigid rules. But, sometimes, when he was angry with me, he told stories about how nice it was in the Children's Home, and how someday he would go back to Russia. But not yet, he usually assured me.

Sometimes, he did seem to be homesick. After all, he had left a whole way of life behind, and he missed the people he had grown to know. At those times, right before he and Panda went to bed, Dima asked to snuggle down with Panda and watch our old videotape of Syktyvkar. He would occasionally tell me stories about the children. There was Irma Krasney who was afraid of dogs. When she saw a dog she would huddle up and shiver, he said. And then of course there was Nadia. "I don't know how I would have made it through without her," Dima told me one night. In his typically adult way, he seemed to grasp things that many grown-ups don't understand.

I once asked Dima, as I gave him and Panda a kiss goodnight, if the women who cared for the children in Syktyvkar kissed them good night and tucked them in.

"No, Mama, they didn't," he said, looking at me as though I didn't grasp even the simplest of things, that the answer was obvious. Then he thought about it for a minute and said, "You know, I don't know why they never did that. I guess they didn't want to," he said, dismissively.

I remember the feel of those first few months so vividly, in part because I had to write reports and send them back to our adoption agency, World Child, and in part because they carried such an emotional impact. I remember them in the way people remember where they were when John Kennedy was shot, or when the World Trade Center went down.

It was a time when Dima was still a mystery to us and we looked forward to each new day with eager anticipation, hoping to learn more who our son would be and what kind of family we would form. It was a time before we even knew what the problems would be, and how we would solve them. It was also a time when we were still inextricably bound to Syktyvkar, bound to send reports back, bound to send pictures back.

Apparently, the international adoption laws were being hammered out in Russia during this time period, and the pro-adoption groups wanted to prove the children were really being sent to better situations and needed pictures to circulate. Since Dima was one of only a small group of children adopted from Russia at that point in time, I was getting frequent requests for photographs. Dima's adjustment not only had implications for our family, but to a certain extent for adoption in Russia.

So I have records of these early times, reports and pictures. It was impossible to convey through these reports the way I felt about him, the intense connection I had with him. And photographs didn't tell the whole story either, but at least choosing pictures to include was the easy part. There was a lot to take pictures of that spring, because every day was an adventure, a foray into some wild, unexpected land. I would thumb through our packs of pictures and consider our evolving life together. There was a picture of Dima on his little green bicycle. I knew that Tatiana and Galina would be thrilled that Dima had such a luxury as a bicycle, but even more than that, that he could ride a bicycle despite his leg problems. They would remember the first day they had met him, when he was just out of surgery and had never walked before.

But I would remember something very different as I looked at Dima's image. In the picture, Dima has on a bicycle helmet and is sitting on a little green bicycle, the one that had appeared in the garage shortly after he had looked so longingly at the family bicycles. Although my husband had put training wheels on it so Dima could ride it right away, Dima was determined to ride independently. My husband would painstakingly work with him, teaching him how to ride. I had watched quietly from the window as my 53 year-old husband ran alongside Dima, who was wobbling around our yard on his bicycle. Every day for weeks the two of them went out and Dima practiced and fell, practiced and fell until finally, proudly, delightedly, Dima showed me that he had mastered riding his bicycle. And that's what I thought about, as I slipped the picture of Dima on his little bicycle into the envelope.

And then there is the great picture of Dima missing his front teeth, with his adult teeth beginning to come in, vampire style over the gums. I remembered vividly when he lost that baby tooth, a small front tooth that left in its wake an empty spot in the front of his mouth, marked by a small drop of blood. He came to me pointing at the small, red toothless spot on his gum while holding out his tooth. I smiled.

"You and Panda will have to put it under your pillow," I said.

Dima looked at me as though I had lost my mind.

I asked him what he had done before when he had lost teeth in Syktyvkar.

"Oh," he said, "the women gave me a tissue and carefully, carefully hold it there," he said gesturing to his gum.

"And what about the teeth?" I asked.

He shrugged. "They threw them away."

"Well, we'll put the tooth under your pillow. Panda can help you. The tooth fairy will come and take it. She'll leave you some money for it."

"Really? Money?" He was intrigued. Later on, when he had more language, he spent days asking questions about what the tooth fairy looked like. "Is she like a little animal, like a squirrel?" he asked. "What does she do with the teeth? Where does she get the money?"

I expected him to ask what rate of exchange she was able to get for foreign money. He finally came up with the theory that the tooth fairy needed to take the teeth to bring them to the little babies so they would have teeth of their own.

He explained it to me in a very adult voice, "See it,

Mama, if the tooth fairy doesn't bring the little babies teeth, what are they going to do? They won't be able to chew their food; they need those teeth." He also was ecstatic about the money the tooth fairy left. He showed Panda in the morning the money under his pillow.

"Got any teeth, Panda?" he asked. But, alas, Panda lost no teeth that summer. I hid Dima's baby teeth in a secret compartment of my desk and collected all of them. From time to time I would look at them and feel again a sense of relief that I had Dima safe with me.

And there was the picture of Dima holding a pink ice cream cone. To most anyone else, this was just a typical American kid on a hot summer night. But I kept remembering when we first brought Dima to a special ice cream parlor that he sat on the edge of his seat in the car, squealing "*Maroshenoye! Maroshenoye!*" He had heard of children in Russia having pink ice cream cones to lick, had even perhaps seen them on the streets as he marched with his little group back to a meal of tea and sausage, but certainly it had not been something within his experience. When we got to the ice cream shop Dima looked at the pictures of the cones with all kinds of colors and flavors and toppings, and looked up at me, a smile creeping across his entire face. Who could believe such a store existed? This was certainly a land filled with pleasures one could barely have imagined. My husband and I watched, trying hard not to look at each other and break out laughing, as Dima frantically tried to catch the drips from an ice cream cone with his tongue, trying as hard as he could to keep it from melting all over him.

There were even pictures of Dima and Franklin taken together, caught at rare moments of peace. Although the weekends were still difficult, there were increasingly long periods of time that they played together without mayhem. They were even getting to a point where they could watch television together without kicking each other. Actually, they were starting to become friends, and Franklin was starting to watch out for Dima.

But my pictures, my observations, were all of Dima's new

life, and didn't come close to telling the whole story. Dima's life didn't start in our family and his memories of Russia didn't end when he walked off the plane and handed the immigration officer his packet. He had had his own life before us, and he thought of it often in that early time. He was sometimes homesick for the orphanage and the people he knew there.

Once, when Dima told me how he missed the "children of Syktyvkar," we put on the tape I had received so long before we adopted Dima. He and I sat together watching this same film, with its glimpses of Nadia and Dima, and the same stern Russian women. And sometimes Dima sat in the darkened television room, watching this film by himself, over and over.

It was right after this that it suddenly occurred to me that Galina and Tatiana were only a phone call away. Although I thought of Syktyvkar as so far away, we were inextricably connected. Syktyvkar was not on another planet, was not out of reach; it would be nothing, really, to call. Galina and Tatiana had been the only adults who were constant in Dima's life. I talked to Svetlana who agreed that it would be relatively simple to call Syktyvkar, and that it would be a good idea.

I made a list of things for Svetlana to tell Galina and Tatiana, bragging things about how he could ride a bicycle, swim and sail. And I had some questions, too. For instance, I wondered what had happened to Nadia.

And so, a short time later, we placed the call and quickly got through to a very surprised Galina. Svetlana talked with her for a while and then put Dima on for a few minutes. Dima refused to talk in Russian. He listened to the voices on the phone, said "*da*" a few times, and quickly handed the phone to Svetlana who gracefully interceded.

When she got off the phone she told me Tatiana was excited that Dima was riding a bicycle. "We didn't think such a thing was possible because of his leg problems," she had said.

Ah, but in America, anything is possible!

They were relieved to hear he was doing well. They were worried about how he would adjust, and had heard, as we had all heard, that some children were not adjusting.

They also told Svetlana how things were changing in

Russia. The economics were even worse, their lives even harder, but it was becoming possible to travel.

"Who knows, someday, we may even visit America." At the time it seemed inconceivable, and yet it planted a fantasy in my mind of a possible future visit. What would she find if she came here? What, I wondered, would we be able to make out of our little rag-tag family?

"And Nadia?" I asked. "Is Nadia still there?"

"I asked about Nadia. There is a summer program for children to go to, and she is there now. But in the fall, she will go to the next children's home. I could tell from Tatiana's voice she was resigned. There is no choice." Svetlana said.

"And," Svetlana said, "send more pictures."

I looked at the envelope I had ready to mail, already thick with photographs and thought, surely I must have pictures of everything in there. But I decided to take one more look through my box of pictures to see if there was anything that was missing. And there, in the last picture, is Dima, holding on to Panda Puppet, and I knew no packet would be complete without a picture of Panda.

I was worried about Dima's adjustment, after hearing about the problems many of the children had, but he seemed so connected that I remained hopeful. It was still difficult to try and make things flow smoothly on the weekends, but the boys were certainly starting to get along better. We were still trying to figure out how to make the whole family relationship work when Franklin unexpectedly came to live with us full time.

"My mother said she can't take care of me right now and it's better for me to be here," he reported to us when he came one weekend for a visit. He then set up his Sega, a gift from his grandfather, in his new bedroom. He politely asked for a blanket, and neatly folded his few clothes into a drawer.

It's hard to convey the lightning speed with which this all happened. It wasn't as though we all got to sit down, discuss and plan this. And for me, I went from having no children to having two children, both of whom had suffered severe dislocations in their lives, in just a matter of months. We were all reeling with the suddenness of events. As I look back at this, I realize that Franklin took these events with amazing calm and tried as best he could to fit in. At the time, I was trying so hard to make sure that Dima would be able to adjust, I didn't realize how mature a child Franklin really was and how easily he settled in, considering the circumstances.

It wasn't long after this that I had an opportunity to hear Franklin's feelings about his new home. He came to me one afternoon, when he was nine, with a paper he had earnestly drafted on the computer. The title was *The Kids Bill of Rights*. It said:

I believe kids have the rights of an adult. These rights are to:

A kid has a right to a good education

No hitting a kid

No getting mad at a kid if he accidentally does something wrong

A kid has a right to have food and a place to stay

Give a kid a home

A kid has a right to not get yelled at if he doesn't do anything wrong

A kid has a right to have some stuff to play with

A kid has a right to have a chance to talk about stuff

I held my breath for a moment when I read it, wondering what this was all about. Who could argue with any of that?

"Well, what do you think?" I asked him, "Are your rights being upheld here?"

"Oh, yes," he said. "I'm perfectly satisfied." I breathed a sigh of relief. We were going in the right direction. A few more steps that way, and I'd have this parenthood thing nailed - maybe. But still the situation was complicated and required good will and a sense of humor and perspective from everyone. Looking back, I think we had that!

The night Franklin moved in, Dima had had a little talk with me. He'd never met Franklin's mother, but he did know Franklin's Aunt Lauren. He liked her, as we all did. But he explained that if I got sick and couldn't take care of him, he didn't think he should go live with Aunt Lauren.

"See it," he said, "her house is too small. It wouldn't be

right." He had no real understanding of how or why Franklin was in our family, but he began to worry. He worried that just as Franklin's mother couldn't take care of him, perhaps something would happen to me and he, Dima, would be forced to move. Perhaps because of all the dislocations in his life, coupled with his early experiences of long periods spent in a hospital environment, Dima became obsessed with the concept of dying.

He was keenly aware of the benefits of having a mother, and he worried a lot about what would happen to him if I died. We talked about it and I explained to him that if I died Daddy would take care of him, and if we both died, my sister's daughter, his cousin Debbie would take care of him. He nodded solemnly. He liked Cousin Debbie and pointed out to me one of the benefits of this: she had a really cool fast red car with retractable headlights, and he was sure she would let him ride in it. However, he felt it definitely wasn't a good idea for me to die.

"I don't think you're taking this dying stuff seriously enough," he said. "You may not know it, but it's really important for me to have a Mama. Think about it and try not to die. It's more important than you think."

I didn't know whether to laugh or cry. I promised I would try not to die.

"Mama," he said, "I know you keep telling me that if you die you'll go to another world, and I'll keep you in my heart. But what really happens when a person dies?" he persisted.

I told him that people had different ideas of what happened when you died, that no one knew for sure. My own theory, I told him, was that your soul goes on to another life. I told him about raindrops, how the raindrop comes from the clouds, but when it goes through the air it is a drop with a shape and life of its own. When it lands, it becomes part of something bigger than itself, a lake or ocean. Then it evaporates, becomes part of a cloud and starts a new cycle. He nodded solemnly and I thought that that was the end of the conversation.

However, several days later he and Franklin were watching Star Trek together and I heard Dima say, "Franklin, when you die and go to another world, do you want to be a Vulcan or a Pherengi?"

Franklin considered this for a while and discussed the benefits of being a Vulcan, while I rolled my eyes. Obviously my first attempt at some sort of spiritual instruction had failed miserably. But I was new to parenthood and doing my best. The Star Trek "lives after death" discussions continued for months.

CHAPTER 10

With Stories of His Own

Young children often have difficulty accessing their feelings. Drawing allows them to experience their feelings, rather than having to verbalize them. It is a way for them to call attention to a topic that is personally important to them. It helps children explore conflicts and gain control over the way they perceive their lives.[14]

*A*lthough at first most of Dima's activities were solitary play, or play with Franklin, that involved toys and drawings, gradually he began to move out into the community. During this period of time, Dima had begun school for real now and it began to have a major role in his life. Initially going to school was exciting for him. On the first day he had been thrilled about getting on the yellow school bus. That first morning, he explained to me, "I'm sorry Mama but you can't come with me this time. See it, this is for children. You know how you do some things with your friends? Well, this is same thing."

He had gotten on the bus, a small brave figure in his jeans jacket, Nike high top sneakers and red pack. I remember vividly that he turned at the top step, waved to me, and headed onto the bus.

The first day was a roaring success. Joanne later told me that Dima comforted children who were not yet used to school. After all, he had been there for a bit in the spring and knew everyone. He organized a group of boys who built elaborate garages and buildings out of blocks, and was generally pretty satisfied. But, as always, the noise bothered him, and he put his hands over his head, complaining, "It's too loud."

Dima's behavior was never really a problem, although he was included in Joanne's sticker group, which was a small group of four or five children, mostly boys, who got a sticker in the morning and a sticker in the afternoon, if their behavior was appropriate. Joanne assured me that this was just to help keep him on track, nothing to worry about. And it was true, for all his traumatic experiences, he seemed no more distractible or rambunctious than the next kindergartner.

When he did, on rare occasions, get into trouble, he took it hard. One day he came home from school grumpy, flung his red pack on the floor and headed directly over to the television set.

I noticed that there was no afternoon sticker on his shirt. "Bad day at Black Rock?" I asked, trying to hug him. "I see you don't have your sticker. Problem at school?"

He drew himself up to his full height, and said in a tone of exaggerated patience, "Mama, it's a very long story and I don't really want to discuss it." With that he stormed out of the room.

I got to hear his version a little later. He hit Jacob "velly" hard in the stomach by accident, Jacob got angry and threw him on his ear in the snow bank, and the teacher got "velly, velly", angry at both of them. There would be no sticker for him that day!

But, despite minor glitches and a strong personality, kindergarten seemed to be going well. Joanne, who loved him dearly, would call me from time to time with funny anecdotes. One day, shortly after the school held their annual Dinosaur Dig Night, she called with a catch in her voice.

Dinosaur Dig Night had been a fantastically inventive evening, attended by both parents and children. The sandbox was set up with piles of fresh sand with dinosaur bones hidden in it so that families could dig for bones together. After the dig was finished, there was a buffet meal of dishes the children had cooked, all with dinosaur themes. Joanne told me she was calling to tell me what Dima said the next day when she had asked the children what they liked best about Dinosaur Night. While most of the children answered that they liked digging in the sand and finding bones, or liked some special food, Dima had told her very earnestly, "What I liked best was that I had a Mama and Daddy to come to Dinosaur Dig Night."

And, during that time, I began to get more and more glimpses of who Dima really was and what he thought about, worried about. I knew that Dima had had a lot to cope with in his past, but I still didn't know what he'd experienced. I sometimes encouraged him to tell me stories from the orphanage, especially when we would sit together and have our snack before bedtime, but he would wave me away. He didn't like to talk about those times, he told me. And of course, at least initially his language skills weren't really up to the task.

I think that part of the problem in coaxing him to talk about emotional times was that young children usually have an easier time showing their feelings through play or through drawings, rather than discussing them. One reason is that they haven't yet integrated the areas of their brains that deal with emotions with the areas that deal with language, and it is really difficult for them to discuss feelings. So, I stocked his play area with a sand table, little people dolls, a dollhouse, paints – all the things that would make it easy for him to play out his worries.

And stories began to emerge. The one about the three mean big boys would come up over and over in different ways. One day we were playing in the sandbox with a bunch of toys and some dolls and there was a baby doll right nearby. The situation was too perfect; I couldn't help myself. I moved the baby closer, within view of Dima. He took it. Immediately he set up an elaborate story. The three boys were mean. They teased the baby all the time because they hated him so much. They threw him off a bridge and broke his leg. Dima carefully wrapped a tissue around the baby doll's leg, so that it looked like it was wearing a cast. The baby with its leg bound in a cast would often appear in Dima's stories and play from then on. He put the baby in the hospital and explained solemnly that the mother couldn't stay in the hospital. The baby had to wait there for his mother to come. That theme would come up again and again.

I knew that play could be used not only to help children express feelings but to help them feel more in control of their environment. Virginia Axline had pioneered the concept of nondirective play therapy, and in her approach there was no attempt to direct the child's play or interfere in any way with it in any way. The idea was to make the child feel safe and feel control over the immediate environment, in order to explore his or her own ideas. The adult listened and clarified the child's ideas, validating the idea that the child has the ability to solve his or her own problems. I took this approach, and I just listened and sometimes summarized his stories for him, without comment. I knew that if any child could work things out for himself, it was Dima.

But doll families were not his only interest. One afternoon, just as I had snuggled down on the living room couch to read a good book, I glanced in the direction of the fireplace and found myself eye to eye with a little green army man poised to kill. It turned out that he was flanked by companions, all camouflaged, all with weapons raised and all ready to shoot the enemy, whoever that might be. Lately, it seemed that every time I opened a cupboard, or moved a book, an armed green man fell from his post.

The soldiers belonged to Dima, although I hadn't bought them for him. I resolutely brought home nurturing, wholesome toys designed to stimulate creativity. He had shelves stacked with Lego's, with blocks, with paints and clay. But every time he got his two-dollar allowance, he pleaded with me to take him to the dollar store, where he would buy two packages of the small green plastic figures.

At first, I had tried to dissuade him from buying these with his allowance, but soon capitulated. I told him that I wouldn't buy weapons for him, but if he wanted to spend his own money on them, that would be his choice. He didn't hesitate a beat, and would smile with satisfaction as he gave the clerk his money.

From that moment on, he embarked on his massive collection of army men. The dollar bags added up, and gradually, I adjusted to this. I couldn't help but be fascinated by his play. After all, I had done play therapy for years and I knew there was no clearer window into my child's soul than watching him play quietly, acting out stories.

So I watched, mesmerized as Dima dragged out both his block set and his canisters of army men. First, he would build elaborate structures with his blocks. Usually he built aircraft carriers, but sometimes he just built forts and cities. The carriers usually had many levels, and little hidden spaces in them. When he was finished building his structure, he would spend hours positioning his army men, getting them just so. If I showed even the slightest interest, he would explain their weaponry, what each one could do, how they backed each other up, how they hid in the small spaces he had created.

"They look really powerful," I said, taking a wild stab at the issues. I knew that feeling powerless and out of control were big issues for most kids who'd lived with uncertainty and dislocations in their lives.

"Well," he said, "they are. But that's not really the point."

"Oh?" I said.

"Yes, the point is, they can protect you. Like from invasion. It's important to protect yourself."

"I'm sure it is," I said.

He looked at me evenly, as though he thought I was being condescending. "You may not know it, but there are a lot of really bad people in the world. You really have to take care of yourself." Then he turned back to his army men to signal that our discussion was through.

As the military play continued, Franklin began to join in some of Dima's play. The blocks and army men took over the entire house, at least in the beginning. My husband and I spent many evenings overhearing the boys discussing the carriers and forts they were building, listening as little by little, they began to cooperate in their building ventures. Sometimes they would run over to us and say with pride, "Look what we built!" and we would look at each other silently, and smile. And we both watched with satisfaction as the army men began to give way to less militaristic toys. I breathed a sigh of relief when Dima began to seem less focused on protecting himself, and on creating small hiding spaces. I hoped he was beginning to feel safer.

Dima also loved to draw, from the very beginning. Drawings have been used throughout history to tell stories. Psychologists have long been interested in children's drawings for what they tell about the child's fears, hopes and perceptions about the world. In addition to being a method for children to express themselves, drawing has also been used to assess emotional and cognitive development in children.[15] Interpretations often are associated with over or under emphasis of a given body part. Omitting a body part, such as the legs, often indicates anxiety about that part. Long arms are considered a desire to reach out to others, while small arms point to a child feeling powerless. Aggressive children draw teeth and make the hands into claws more often than timid children.[16]

As Dima began to draw more and more, his drawings changed markedly. His early drawings show people who have only flowing robes on, with no visible legs. They were rudimentary figures, with unelaborated features, more typical of the drawings a child much younger might make. Those drawings were interesting in a number of ways. The school psychologist who initially evaluated Dima's skills commented on his drawings of people and thought they indicated that he had significant anxiety about his legs. The only other child she had ever seen draw people with robes instead of legs had been a child confined to a wheelchair.

I had noticed that he never drew people's legs, and agreed with her theory, although personally I thought his drawings were unusually charming. He also drew people without hands and there are many volumes written about the meaning of that, including the fact that children deprived of touching and affection often draw people in that way.

But I put all that aside for a while and didn't think too much more about it until about a year later, when Dima finally started bringing home drawings showing people with legs. Suddenly the robes were gone, and people wore pants and skirts and showed their legs. And over the next year, the details on his drawings changed markedly. The drawings began to look much more typical of a child his own age than a younger child. Sometime during that time, Dima drew an Olympic ice skater with huge muscular legs, which thrilled me so much that I framed it and hung it in the living room.

"Just look at the legs on that skater," I beamed. Our visitors usually looked at me with bewilderment, and tried to be politely enthusiastic about the picture, missing its significance.

Soon after, I bought a scrapbook to keep Dima's drawings and often, while we had our afternoon snack, he would make pictures of airplanes and carriers, space ships, mammoth battles being waged on one planet or another. I would look at his pictures and think that some of his concerns are not so different from that of any child his age. But, once in a while, I would be brought up short with the realization that his artwork reflected his early experiences and he had a whole other life to consider.

One night, as I was propped up in bed, reading late, Dima came into my room, looking shaken and distraught. "I had a nightmare, Mama, a terrible one. It seemed so real," he said, plaintively.

"Come sit next to me, tell me your dream," I said. "Here, you can snuggle for a little while, until you feel calmer."

"I don't think I'm going to feel calm again. I was in a ship, a destroyer. A submarine hit it. It started to sink. But that wasn't the worst part. I was in a little room, and I was supposed to go to the bottom of the boat. The bottom of the boat was awful. Terrible things were happening. It was like being in hell." His voice was soft, and he blinked back tears as he said this. He was too upset to tell me more, and sat quietly next to me, thinking his dream over, trying to calm himself.

It was quiet in my room, with only the clock ticking. My husband was not home that night. I could see that Dima couldn't reach any more words. Finally I said to him, "Maybe you can draw this dream for me." I had never asked him to do this before.

He looked relieved. "I think I will," he said. We went into the kitchen and got a drawing pad and pencil, and I made some hot tea.

He began to draw. The pictures flowed from him. He drew boats, destroyers, alien space ships. This was a very involved dream. He took his time, explaining in detail how the alien ships landed at Antarctica. I'm sure this piece of the dream was from a movie he had recently seen. Then the dream skipped to the boat he was on. The part that I paid the most attention to was his drawings of the people in his damaged boat. He was in the bottom of the boat, in a small room. In the next room were three big boys, holding what he called towels, but which looked like clubs. Next to them were two smaller boys, with their tongues hanging out of their mouths.

"See those boys?" he whispered hoarsely, pointing to the big boys. "They are big mean teenagers. They are hurting the littler children because those children are too nice. Look," he said, almost paralyzed with fear, "they have pulled out the tongues of those boys. And they are hitting them with towels. The towels have turned into clubs."

This, I take it, was the real point of his dream. While this was a complicated dream, with implications that made me shudder, just drawing this dream, and talking about it, made him calmer. Big children, the three big boys in the hospital, had figured in Dima's stories and dreams, over and over.

We sat there for quite a while, sipping our tea as he shaded in his picture. Finally he said, "You know, I feel much better. You really are the best mother in the world." He looked at me evenly and said, "You really understand me."

I don't often get this praise. It was one of those moments that as a parent, I live for - to do something just right, to reach a perfect level of communication. And, indeed, after this conversation, after our discussion about the little children who didn't end up well, Dima's level of cooperation soared. A new calm came over him.

I'm sure that, in part, the calm came from being able to talk about his fears, but I think it was also that a realization that he was not only loved, but also understood came to him.

There is a Chinese myth that often circulates in the adoption world and in this myth people who are meant to be together in this world are connected before birth by an invisible red cord. If there was truth to that myth, then I was sure Dima and I had been connected in that way. I continued to feel this sense of connection as our life continued, mostly in more mundane ways and with less drama than the drawing incident.

But one of the more tangible ways Dima's connections to us was reinforced that first year involved his citizenship status, his connection to his new country. Later on, adopted children would automatically get the citizenship status of their new parents, but in the early 1990s citizenship had to be applied for. It was part of the process, the next step of becoming a true American Guy, a citizen.

Dima was still connected to Russia, and would always be. I was relieved that he would be a citizen finally because his adoption had taken place wholly in Russia and been conducted in a mysterious foreign language, filed with a government on the brink of destruction, teetering on the edge. The documentation was, in my mind, somehow suspect, not substantial. When I brought Dima home for the first time, it occurred to me that there were no records of him anywhere, except in the Office of Immigration and Naturalization Service, and that office seemed to be totally unapproachable. The agency had one of those recorded phone messages where you were bombarded with scads of phone menu options, the last one being to speak to an operator. But if you chose that option you found yourself out of the loop, hearing the phrase, "Thank you for calling, have a good day," and then *click*. So I never called them.

But one day out of the blue, or so it seemed, the phone rang and a voice said, "Hello, I'm calling from the Office of Immigration and Naturalization."

Oh, God, I thought, and for a moment my heart sank. If these people I could never get a hold of were calling me, it must be really horrible. Perhaps there were problems with his paperwork. Images of people coming to try and take my child away flashed through my head.

But the woman continued, cheerfully, "We're having a citizenship ceremony for children next month. You applied for his citizenship and we'd like to invite Dima since he will be eligible then."

And then I remembered that I, who rarely completed any paperwork except under duress, who procrastinated about everything, had actually completed the paperwork for Dima's citizenship at the first possible moment. I was convinced the Russian government could change their minds at any minute and snatch him back.

And he was part of a long chain of my family members who got their citizenship here. The INS call triggered visions of my ancestors coming to the United States, some to Ellis Island, wiping tears away as they saw the Statue of Liberty and knew they had arrived, at last, at their new home. Mawkish scenes from all the great epic novels about coming to America flashed through my mind.

Citizenship had been a much-discussed event in my childhood. The story of the immigrant experience was part of the fabric of my childhood, had seeped into my blood. My grandparents' generation had fled horrors of all kinds: Cossacks, pogroms, the ethnic hatreds in Europe brewing under the surface in the early part of the century. I could remember stories passed from mouth to mouth about hiding in barns, hiding in streams, breathing through reeds, fleeing the old country, always with an eye toward the new. And members of my parents' generation were thrilled to be here, ready to cast off any reminders that they had come from someplace besides this glorious, rough and ready country. And the final step, the *piece de resistance,* was to become a full-fledged American citizen at the first available opportunity, and never look back.

Of course, by the time my generation came along, we viewed the whole process with a more jaundiced eye, having been disillusioned by the Vietnam War, among other things. But still, I could feel in my bones the import of this event. I could picture my mother helping friends who barely spoke English fill out their citizen application forms. I could hear her voice as she made calls to find out where night school classes were being held so she could drive people to class, to get them on the road to citizenship. It was an honor and a privilege not to be taken lightly.

And Dima's ceremony, according to the woman from the INS, was not to be the stuffy bureaucratic event usually foisted on adults. No, this was to be an extravaganza, a spectacular, hosted by area school children. It was held to honor and welcome the children getting their citizenship, children who arrived in this country not so long ago, most from places on the globe in turmoil, most here to join their new families.

We had wanted to make sure Dima had some understanding of what all this was about. "You're going to be a citizen," we told him.

"Citizen," he repeated not having a clue as to what we were talking about. He did know it was something good, and smiled.

I didn't have any idea of how to explain it, and so I did what people in my family always did when faced with the incomprehensible; I got a book from the library. It was the tried and true way of dealing with anything; it was the only way my mother even broached the mysterious topic of sex with me. "Here, read this. If you have any questions, you can ask."

So we all trotted down to the library and picked out several picture books on becoming a citizen. Dima especially loved one of the books, a book with bright colors, unraveling the glories of citizenship. He brought it to school with him, and showed his teacher, Joanne, and the other children. He dramatically laid it out for them to feast their eyes, but told them seriously it was a "no touch" item.

Joanne called me that night, and described the whole scene to me. Dima apparently took out a little chair and set it in the middle of the circle, and in a very teacher like way, proceeded to show the other children the pages of the coming to

America book, explaining each picture to them, and showing the book around the whole circle. He was prepared.

Since this was to be an event, my sister came all the way from Washington, D.C.

"Auntie Barbara is coming, Auntie Barbara is coming," Dima ran around the house singing.

A person couldn't show up at such an event in just plain everyday street clothes. The approaches to the appropriate attire for this event were as varied as the parental and cultural backgrounds. Some parents dressed their children in the ceremonial attire of their native country for this event, while others aspired to dizzying heights of patriotic symbolism.

Since I don't sew, and wasn't sure what Russian ceremonial attire was, I opted for Fourth of July gauche. I managed to find a truly remarkable shirt with red and blue stripes on a white background that actually would have been stunning for the event. However, although Dima had been primed on this, at the last minute he changed his mind, and ten minutes before we were about to leave for the ceremony decided he had to wear a tie like Daddy. I wound up putting him in his dress up blue pants, a crisp white shirt, a red power tie and red suspenders. I did hear someone whisper, as he made his way to the stage, that he looked like a six-year-old executive. They were right; he did.

I'm not sure what being a citizen meant for Dima, but he did want to blend into his new life. One of Dima's citizenship gifts was a deep blue glass globe with beautiful stars on it.

"Look" he said, tracing the stars with his fingers, watching the patterns the light made shining through the blue glass. "The stars are all connected through the glass. Kind of like all the people in the world I'm connected to."

I smiled; it was like him to put this idea so poetically. And it was true; Dima was connected to people all over the universe. Sometimes people would ask me what I felt about changing his culture, what responsibilities I felt to keep his heritage and roots. It wasn't a question that resonated with me. Although Dima's world had shifted when we adopted him, and he had stronger and more stable connections than he had before, he was truly still a world child, with roots in

Russia, a childhood in America, and friends from all over the world. And I felt we are all world children: we could appreciate where we came from, we could appreciate the group we were now part of, but our identity was not dependent on that.

CHAPTER 11

Catching Up or on Another Bus?

Dyslexia is the puzzling contradiction between a child's general competent intellectual functioning and the child's inability to master reading skills.[17] Functional MRIs show a difference in the brains of people with dyslexia compared to normal readers.

hroughout the fall that year we were charmed by Dima's personality, and thrilled at how fiercely he was connecting to us. Even though he was fitting in well at school, we couldn't help but notice that some areas were a struggle for him; despite his ease of getting along with people, there were hints of problems to come.

I had watched as he struggled to remember the letter sounds. Joanne had a game called Detective Clipboard. Every day the children got a letter, an A or an M, or a P, something. They were then supposed to be detectives and find things that began with the sound of that letter during the course of the day. Joanne diligently went over the sound with them in the morning before they began their search. This was not a particularly difficult task for most of the children, and, certainly, Dima completed many other seemingly more difficult tasks. However, this game was totally beyond him. He could remember the letter names, but he couldn't seem to remember the sounds, or connect them with anything. I mentioned it to Joanne at the time, but she had waved me away. "Give him a chance, he's just learning the language," she said.

And yet I knew there was more to it. Dima's learning patterns followed the classic lines of a specific reading disability. For example, although he had trouble remembering what sounds went with what letters, he could remember anything he saw. There are defining moments in life, when, in an instant, you come to know the truth of something. I had such a moment when I tried to teach Dima our telephone number. I told him the numbers, tried to help him with some strategies for grouping them, remembering them. He was completely frustrated. It was beyond him. But all of a sudden his face lit up with an idea. He took my hand and said, "Come, Mama," and led me over to our telephone. We had a touch-tone telephone with the buttons laid out in the traditional rows. He looked at the phone.

"Show me," he said, sweeping his hand over the phone. I was startled, but I dialed our number, pushing the pattern of buttons. He watched intently, as he always did. After I showed him the pattern of our phone number, he copied it.

"Was that right?" he asked. It was. What was impossible for him to learn auditorially in many tries, he did visually in one attempt. It was a pattern I would see over and over again when I watched him try to master anything new. He could remember anything he could visualize.

It was some time after this, after he had been home with us for a long enough time to have mastered English, we were watching television when an advertisement came on that talked about the earth's weight. Dima looked at the picture of the earth floating in space and said to me, "You can't weigh the earth."

"Why not?" I asked, absentmindedly. I thought he would say something about no scales being big enough.

"Because," he answered, "you get weight from gravity, from a pull from the earth. The earth can't pull itself. It's floating in space."

My husband looked up from his newspaper. I think we were both a little unnerved by this comment.

"I guess you have to talk about mass, not weight, huh, Dima," my husband said.

Dima nodded solemnly. And yet, that night, when I tucked him into bed and read with him, I was again reminded how difficult it was for him to grasp the idea of sounding out words, to match letters and their sounds. I remember vividly that the first sentence had the word "good" in it, a word he had, by that time, seen hundreds if not thousands of times. I know that because I had personally sat through most of that reading! He looked at it as though it was a foreign assortment of letters, as though the letters had no relationship to anything in the world he was familiar with.

"Good," I finally prompted. He noticeably relaxed.

"Good," he read, as I sank back on the pillow, in despair, thinking of all the reading disabled children I worked with throughout the years, and knowing how difficult life could be for them.

Eventually these learning patterns came to play a major part in Dima's school life. At first his ideas were so imaginative and grown up, and his willingness to express himself so great, that all his language idiosyncrasies were chalked up to English being a second language. He was able to express his feelings and thoughts in an adult way, with some degree of eloquence, despite the fact that his syntax remained garbled and he continued to transpose parts of words. But by the middle of the school year, Dima's English was still noticeably different from standard English. The ideas were always sophisticated, but the phrasing or the tenses were always a little bit off.

Sometimes I thought back to that first report, that discussion with the psychologist in Galina's little office so long ago and many miles away. It was all there, between the lines. He had known almost no words by age five, had years of little language stimulation, had numerous ear infections. And yet, everyone felt that he was so bright, that he would do well.

I didn't say much but I watched, and I knew. When I watched Dima cover his ears when there was just the slightest bit of background noise, and say, "It's too loud," I winced. And when I heard him say often, even after he'd been here a very long time, "I didn't did it," I knew. And when I watched him solve a very complicated problem, or explain seriously the specific details of certain aircraft, I knew that even that was no guarantee that he would be able to learn to read with ease. But still, for a long time, I hoped it wouldn't be a problem for him. I figured even though I could help him cope with reading difficulties, he didn't need one more challenge in his life.

Because Dima started his school career in a small, innovative school setting where the teachers loved him, and the children were wonderful to each other, school wasn't a problem.

I would walk into his school and see children sitting in tents, reading to each other, surrounded by shelves of interesting, beautiful books. The school had no basal readers (those bland books filled with stories of Dick and Jane), no worksheets, no phonic lessons. Reading was treated as an exciting activity, an entrance to magical places. One had only to listen to others read and practice oneself, and doors opened. That is, doors opened for most children. For Dima, the reading door was definitely stuck, perhaps even bolted shut.

The teachers in Dima's small private school really didn't have any specialized strategies to help him, and as the year progressed, Dima still had not picked up any recognizable reading skills. Each time I brought up this worry, the teachers waved it away. "Mother, you are too worried. He'll do fine. He's so smart. And he's only been speaking English for six months." They smiled indulgently at me. I knew they were thinking that I was an overly concerned parent.

Dima enjoyed playing with other children, and especially enjoyed discussion groups, where, I was told, he always had something very insightful to add to the group. He loved competitive games and seemed to hold his own. No one ever teased him, as far as I could tell, although at first I had been concerned about this. After all, he was thin, with big glasses, a frail bone structure, and an idiosyncratic way of speaking. But somehow, his will of iron shone through.

"Tease me?" he repeated incredulously, when I had asked if other children ever gave him a hard time. "I don't allow that. I put a stop to it right away," he said, drawing himself up to his full height, mustering all the dignity he could.

From Dima's perspective school seemed like an ideal place to be if only you didn't have to read and write, and if only the teacher didn't talk so fast. "She talks way too fast," he would tell me almost every night. His teacher didn't talk noticeably faster than anyone else, as far as I could tell.

I pointed this out. I knew that that was often a complaint of children with reading difficulties. The theory was that these children were processing sounds more slowly than others.

"I mean when she gives us directions. Tell her to go slower!" He told me, as though I had God-like powers to alter his environment.

I practiced his word lists with him, and helped him attempt to sound out words. He could, with difficulty, learn basic sight words. Learning vowel sounds, however, was impossible. Dima looked at me like I came from another planet when I tried to teach him the difference between the short "e" sound and the short "o" sound. At first he tried to be patient with me, and humor me. He would pat my hand and say, "Not now, Mama, we'll do it later, if this is something you really want to do."

Eventually, he gave up and told me he just wasn't going to do it. I tried to make reading fun. There were endless games of "sight word bingo," "go-fish phonics," and of course, hours of imaginative bedtime stories, read with my best array of character voices. We even got Panda involved in the process - he was regularly dealt a hand in "go-fish phonics." All to no avail.

And I can remember the advice of friends. "When he wants to read, he will read. When he is ready, he will do it." I, however, knew this was not a readiness issue. It is like telling the parent of a child whose legs are paralyzed that because other children walk when they are ready, their child will too.

Later on, those first silent shadows, those hints of reading difficulties that we had glimpsed in the very beginning of Dima's school career, no longer remained quietly in the background. At some point we transferred Dima to the public school where there was more expertise in specialized reading strategies. However what we gained in instructional methods we lost in nurturing.

"When he comes in here in the morning he wants to socialize," his teacher told me indignantly. "He could get all his board work done if he would only try harder."

Dima had a different take on the situation. "I can't do everything they want me to do in one day. They all go too fast. They rush all the time. I'm getting nervous inside."

When his teachers insisted that he repeatedly miss recess because he hadn't finished his written work, we decided the trade-off wasn't worth it and the following year we sent him back to his little private school. However, this time we arranged to have specialized reading services in place.

Although I didn't think he had a hearing problem, we made an appointment to have his hearing checked, just to rule this out. His hearing turned out to be fine, but I was told he had a lot of scar tissue in his ears, the sign that he had probably had numerous ear infections that had gone undetected as an infant. Sometimes it felt that as I got information about Dima, it was like getting little pieces to a puzzle and all of a sudden a whole section would come together.

Dima began to tell me about early ear infections he had had, infections, which would certainly have compounded the overall effects of limited language stimulation in orphanage settings. There had been no indications in his records of ear infections, and most probably they had gone unnoticed by busy caretakers. However, Dima told me from time to time, that he remembered his ears hurting, remembered not being able to hear much.

"It was like being underwater, Mama," he said. I knew that was the classic description of otitis media, or inner ear infection.

"How long did it last?" I asked him.

"I don't know. It seemed like a long time. Then I would hear again. Then it came back. Off and on."

The pediatrician suggested that he have a further evaluation that would indicate not whether or not he heard sounds, but whether he was processing the sounds he heard effectively. We scheduled an evaluation at Sunnyview Hospital. The evaluation, a central auditory processing assessment, was designed to evaluate how well the child is able to process incoming auditory information.

I explained to Dima in advance that they would give him games to do, puzzles to solve, would ask him to listen to things and repeat them back. He already knew the drill, and he liked doing puzzles, and certainly liked chatting with adults, so he was basically agreeable to this.

"Just not for too long," he said, remembering back to times when he had been sandbagged by being assured there were "just a few more questions to go."

When we arrived at Sunnyview we found the audiologist to be a young, cheerful man, who immediately put Dima at ease. He set Dima up in a small booth with a lot of electronic equipment in front of him. Then he placed a set of earphones on Dima's ears, and Dima grinned. He looked like he was about to pilot his own plane.

The audiologist invited me to sit with him in a place outside the little booth, where I could watch the whole process while he explained what was going on. Dima was given a series of tests. He demonstrated problematic responses on three of the four tasks. The results indicated problems remembering auditory information, especially in remembering the initial information given in a series.

However, there was one piece of information that emerged that was particularly interesting to me. There is a task which involves giving children competing sentences to their right and left ear through the earphones. There is usually what is called a "right ear" advantage because material presented in the right ear goes directly to the left side of the brain where language is organized. When Dima was asked to listen and repeat a sentence heard in his right ear while another sentence was read in the left ear, he struggled with this task. The audiologist sighed and said that since Dima was having such extreme difficulty with the tasks presented in the right ear, there probably wasn't much point giving him the tasks requiring he repeat information given through the left ear. But, as almost an afterthought, the audiologist decided to give him a few of the left ear tasks just to see what happened. Dima whipped through the tasks, getting a hundred percent of them correct. "This is very unusual," the audiologist told me, "although I have read about it before. I don't really know how to explain it, but it probably represents atypical organization of language processing areas."

I knew that children with dyslexia are thought to differ in the brain area in which words are translated from visual symbols into sounds. Dyslexia appears to be a disorder with a genetic basis that affects about five percent of the general population. However, children who have experienced complex trauma have much higher rates of the learning and language disabilities related to dyslexia than the normal population of children.[18]

A television special about children from Eastern European orphanages that I saw shortly after this offered some possible explanations. PET scans were just starting to be used to study the relationship between language disorders and areas of the brain used to process language. Children from orphanages often experience significant language delays related to early language deprivation. It appeared that they didn't develop language areas in their brains in the same way as language stimulated children, and actually may use different areas of their brain for language acquisition.

When we were finished with the test, we went over all the results with the language therapist. To no one's surprise, Dima's score pattern on intellectual testing showed at least normal intelligence but with a tremendous amount of scatter. That is, he did very well on many of the subtests, yet did poorly on others. He excelled, for instance, on those tasks where he had to use his abstract thinking skills to tell how things were alike. Analogies had always been Dima's specialty, even when his English was rudimentary. I can still remember him explaining to me, when he was only six, how he was very hot, "like a hamburger cooking on a grill, Mama," or explaining the vibration of the stereo, "it's like a heart, beating in the wall." When he had to perform at a concert he told me even though he didn't blush like some children did, he was so hot he felt "like a volcano about to explode."

He definitely had a poetic streak. And strangely enough, despite his language issues, Dima knew many difficult vocabulary words. I can remember when he was six years old and only about six months into English, he cautioned me to hold something carefully because it was "very, very, fragile."

And of course, he did well on anything that involved remembering designs, or building with blocks. For as long as I could remember, Dima could hold any design pattern in memory, could copy it, rotate it, turn it upside down - all in his head! And he remembered every detail of anything he saw. He could put all kinds of involved Lego designs together without benefit of directions. So when he had been asked on the tests to copy block designs, or put together puzzles, or discover what was missing in a picture, he could certainly dispatch those tasks with ease.

The conclusion was that Dima was a child with at least normal intelligence, but in addition to some problems related to English as a second language, he also demonstrated a pattern consistent with language processing problems. The therapist pointed out many of those endearing but telltale traits I had already noticed, such as the fact that Dima hated loud noises, and that he took forever to get his thoughts together to begin a sentence. I can remember a friend telling me she knew when it was Dima calling her son because there was always seconds of silence when she first answered. And I know how frustrated he would get when adults wouldn't wait for him to come up with his answer but would rush in to fill the silence.

"But if they only didn't interrupt me, I would have come up with the words," Dima would say plaintively later.

We left Sunnyview feeling that we had a few more pieces to the puzzle. We had learned a little more about Dima, but we weren't sure it would make much difference in his day-to-day learning life.

Dima summed it up more succinctly. "They had a lot of nice machines there, Mama, but I don't want to do that again. Enough is enough."

It was not too long after this when Dima, who was sitting on the floor in his room, building with his blocks, said to me "Mom, I can't read as well as most of the kids in my class. How come?"

I thought for a minute, trying to think of an analogy to use to explain it. Finally I said, "I know reading is hard for you, but reading isn't the whole picture. Reading is a tool, kind of like a shovel. When you build things in the sand, you need a shovel to work with. Everyone needs one. If you don't have a shovel, you have to use your hands and it doesn't work as easily. But what you wind up building doesn't depend on how big or strong the shovel you have is, it depends on your imagination, on your ideas, on your heart. You have great imagination, great ideas, great thoughts. You will build wonderful things with your life."

Dima looked up at me and smiled and then went back to his work, humming happily to himself.

CHAPTER 12

You Don't Have to be Perfect to be in Our Family

Parenthood, whether attained through adoption or not, is an unpredictable journey that changes one's preconceived notions, makes one reconsider what's important in relationships.

I was beginning to understand Dima, the individual who had come into the world with his own assortments of gifts and talents. And we were making the connections of family and community that children and their parents make. But always, when you connect with an older child from a different culture, there are more complicated questions about how we are all connected that lurk under the surface. Some of these questions are related to age-old adoption issues, but some had to do with Dima, his feelings about his new culture and his relationship to the old. He kept his Komi owl on the wall, and wanted to keep his name as Dima because it was Russian just like him. Yet he resolutely refused to speak Russian, even to well meaning Russian friends of ours who coaxed him gently and asked him *Kak de la?*" (how are you?) as he stared silently at the floor.

One quiet afternoon, during a period of time when things seemed to be going especially well, Dima looked up from the floor, where he'd been playing with his Lego toys, and said softly, "You're not my real mother, you know."

A shock wave went through me. I guess that had he said this in a moment of anger, I'd have been prepared, or more prepared at any rate. I stayed quiet for a moment, thinking about what to say, what he meant. I'd read lots of adoption books about talking to your child about this issue, but the usual advice, the usual words, the politically correct phrases, didn't seem to apply.

I settled on a non-committal "Oh?" and held my breath, waiting to see what he would say next.

He continued looking away from me, focusing studiously on his Legos. "Well, I had another mother first. She left me," he added, his voice wavering. "You wouldn't understand," he added.

One of the most unfair parts of parenthood, it seems to me, is that these momentous conversations come out of the blue, when you haven't had a chance to prepare what you want to say. It seemed not long ago that Dima was telling me how he had had another mother who must have died. And, furthermore, he had been telling me how wonderful it was to have me for his mother. But one of the wonders of childhood is that as you grow and develop you understand things in different ways. Dima was trying out different theories, and as he did, his perceptions of how we were all connected changed.

For me, it was a shock. My perceptions weren't changing and I had felt totally connected to him, given over to motherhood from the very beginning. I remembered that moment when I left the orphanage with him, holding his hand. I knew that he was depending on me and I realized that I was all he had in the world. The connections that formed in that moment bound me as tightly as any umbilical cord has ever bound mother and child. I knew whose he was. He was mine.

But those words, *"You're not my real mother"*, gripped me.

I was stunned for a few seconds, but when I recouped, I realized it wasn't about me. It was about him, the losses in his life. I took a deep breath. "I'll try to understand," I said. I wanted to rush in and tell him I was his real mother and all those other platitudes, but I knew, at this minute, they were beside the point. The point was to understand his loss.

"My other family left me," he said. "Never mind. You can't do anything about it anyway."

"I understand you're upset. I understand." I let those words hang in the air for a few minutes. Finally I said, "You don't know what happened, why your birth family couldn't take care of you, and I don't know either. Times were difficult in Russia at the time you were born."

"I don't care. They still left me. Forget it," he said.

I didn't know much about the circumstances that prevented his birth parents from taking care of him, but I had one piece of information I thought he would find somewhat comforting. When I had gotten Dima's papers from Galina there was a small insurance policy in his packet. The Russian administrators commented on the policy; it was unusual for a child in an orphanage to have one. "Someone," they said, "must have really been worried about his future."

The insurance policy would come due when he was eighteen and was for a small amount of rubles. The Russians were surprised he had it, but commented that the amount of rubles would, with all the problems with currency, now only buy him a few loaves of bread at best. But still, I thought someone didn't want him to be totally empty-handed.

I told Dima about this, putting it in a way he could understand. And I said that it must have been extraordinarily difficult for his birth parents to give him to someone else's care. I also added that although I didn't know them, I knew that Dima was such a warm, empathetic person, that I felt in my heart that they must have been good, kind people caught in a terrible predicament.

He shrugged and kept playing with his toys. I knew he heard me. I was sure now that this wasn't the end of the conversation, that I would hear more about it.

And still it left the phrase, "You're not my real mother,"

hanging in the air. Dima loved me. That wasn't the problem. He didn't want to leave me. But he was grappling with understanding exactly who we were to each other, how we were connected. Maybe that's the universal question for all of us, adopted or not.

To some extent, Franklin's presence had complicated this understanding. In the beginning, I told Dima that I was his, Dima's, mother since I was raising him and I loved him so dearly. I was as real a mother as anyone else's; I just wasn't his birth mother. But now, he pointed out, Franklin lived with us, I took care of Franklin and loved him, and yet Franklin had someone else who was his mother. Being a stepparent brought to the fore the issues of how we were all connected. In the end, of course, it would turn out that love and shared experiences were the fibers that connected us.

I realized that although I cared deeply about both boys, being a stepparent full time was different than being a parent. In a way, it must seem odd that the two experiences, which appeared to be almost identical on the surface, were quite different. In both cases, I became the adult responsible, full time, for a child about whom I previously knew little. But the experiences had a different feel to them, and I tried to understand it. As a stepparent, I assumed close to a hundred percent of the day-to-day responsibility and zero percent of the decision-making. When I became Dima's mother, I knew he depended on me, I knew I was responsible for him, and I knew the decisions I made on his behalf would shape his world. But with Franklin, at least initially, I was in no man's land. I had no real rights to make any decisions that affected him because those decisions rightfully belonged to his parents. Of course I had some influence, but still, that is not the same thing. It turned out, though that over time, a lot of that changed and although I had few legal rights, I assumed more and more of a real parental role to Franklin.

I have often thought about my own feelings about bonding to each of the children and have searched for some universal message that sheds light on the mysterious ability people have to connect with each other, to love each other. My feelings of connection with Dima were immediate, whereas my connection with Franklin grew steadily over the years. The stepchild/ stepparent relationship is frequently viewed as a difficult one. One will often hear people say things like, "Well, when it's your own it's different" or, "she treats her *own* child differently." The implication is that the difference of feelings about "your own" and a stepchild has roots in the biological relationship. But I've come to the conclusion from the experience of raising an adopted child and a stepchild, both from the age where they had a life before me that it doesn't have anything to do with biology. When I think about the contrasts in the expectations we have about parenting compared to step parenting, I often think of a story about buying clothes for the first time for my children.

My experience with buying Dima his first new clothes had been a very emotional one, though it had occurred before I had even met him. I had to buy clothes for Dima before I left for Russia, and while it seems like a mundane task, it was the act of buying clothes that made me realize I had a real son out there somewhere in the world. He existed, he had a specific clothes size, and I was buying the first clothes I would ever buy for the first child that would be mine.

The morning I went out to the clothing store, I was clutching a crumpled yellow paper in my hand with the statistics Allison had given me scrawled on it and a list of things Dima would need. I knew that he was 43 inches tall and weighed 40 pounds, but I had no clothes' sizes, no preferences, nothing else on which to go.

The store was quiet the day I was there, and the sun streamed through the skylights. I knew I needed underwear, slacks and shirts in addition to the heavy winter stuff and I began fingering through the racks. There were so many choices - sweatshirts, button-down shirts, and turtlenecks. I didn't know this child, his tastes, his preferences. I would have to get what I liked not what he liked. However, at that time, I figured it wouldn't matter much to him, he'd be excited to have new things. Little did I know what strong opinions he would have on clothing. For example, he didn't like turtlenecks because he didn't like anything constricting on his neck, having had a bad experience in that department. And he would like soft clothing because he was very attuned to fabrics and their feel. However, at that moment I was blissfully ignorant. I did, however, need to figure out sizes.

There was a saleswoman lurking nearby and I told her I needed a little help because I needed to buy some clothing for a child and wasn't sure of the size. I wasn't ready to go into my life's story with a total stranger, and tried to keep things matter of fact. "I need clothes for a six year old," I said.

"Oh, well, is he big for his age? Heavy, thin, average?"

I shrugged. "I'm not really sure." I assumed he was pretty small, but I hadn't ever seen him with other children his age. "Here, he's 43 inches and 40 pounds. What size do you think that'll make him?"

She looked at me a little oddly. "That's about average height, but he must be awfully skinny to weigh only 40 pounds." We decided on a size 5/6 slim, which actually turned out to be right.

Next I went to my list, and we started to discuss styles. I could see I had her curiosity piqued. "Shopping for someone else?" she asked, fishing for clues. "It's always so hard to buy clothes for friends' children."

"Well, actually, it's for me. My son. The child who's going to be my son," I said, spilling out my life story. "I'm adopting a little boy. From Russia."

The saleswoman followed along, with a blank look at first. Then, in a magic moment, she put it all together and became effusive, remarkably helpful.

I explained to her how I was trying so hard to find the right clothes and I had almost no time. In that moment I imagined the little boy who would wear these clothes, thought about his personality, about his likes and dislikes, and who he might be. I got so caught up in the emotion of the moment that I had to fight back tears. Fortunately, I noticed the saleswoman was also fighting back tears, and we became fast partners. In the next two hours I bought pants, shirts, mittens, everything. I even bought Donald Duck and Mickey Mouse underwear, and we both wondered if he'd ever seen cartoons, if he would know who Donald or Mickey were.

I also purchased the last size 5/6 ski jacket in the mall

that day. It was red and black with lots of pockets and zippers. At the time that seemed insignificant; all I cared about was that it was warm. It turned out, however, that the coat was the thing my guy loved most about dressing that cold morning to come with me and leave the orphanage. He pulled the zippers back and forth, looked through all the pockets and was fascinated by the roll-up hood that hid in the collar. He'd never seen anything like it. It was definitely a few points in my favor.

My first experience in shopping with Franklin was in sharp contrast to this. He had been living with us full time since school began in September, and by the end of October it was clear that winter was coming and he needed some warm things. I told him that I would take him shopping and get him, among other things, a winter coat. His grandmother and mother had plans to get that for him, he told me, and they wanted to pick it out themselves. That was okay with me, but as the weeks passed and the weather grew colder, and no coat appeared, I knew it was time for me to get him one. I took him shopping with me and made some suggestions about jackets and coats he might try, ones that looked warm, ones I liked. I saw a particularly colorful ski jacket and said, "Hey, Franklin, I bet you would look really sharp in this. Would you like to try it, do you like it?"

He looked at it doubtfully. "Well, I don't think my mother will like it. I think she'd rather I get something darker, like navy blue. She likes navy blue. Maybe I should try that one," he said, pointing to a rather drab jacket on the rack.

I knew he was nine years old and trying to be obedient and tactful. I said only, "Well, your mother isn't here right now and we're shopping for this jacket, so I think we should just go ahead and make the best choice we can. Sometime, when your mother takes you shopping, then she will help you choose." He looked up at me with concern and chose the navy blue one.

So, despite the parental responsibilities for Franklin, I had, initially, few of the perks. I had room only to fill the narrowest of roles. The expectations and roles Franklin and I had for our relationship were very different than the expectations and roles Dima and I had. Dima wanted a mama, needed a mama and I was there. Frank already had a mama. I felt redundant.

Over the years, though, these feelings steadily changed, and we developed a strong relationship on our own terms. I began to connect to him slowly, began to appreciate the person he was, and enjoy him for what he brought to our family and for who he was. And, it turned out that he was a really remarkable, easy-going person, which made it all that much easier, of course.

Even though I felt totally parental with Dima, clear who we were to each other, I tried to consider it from his point of view. I told Dima how I'd seen him on that tape, fallen in love with him, chosen him, how I always felt that he was meant to be mine. I thought of a story I'd heard about Rosie O'Donnell. When her young son asked about his adoption, she told him that God made a mistake and brought him to the wrong person. That's why she had to go to all the trouble of finding him and adopting him. I loved it. It may not have been politically correct, but it hit a resonant chord.

Dima didn't buy the fact that he was chosen because we saw him on videotape. He told me, scornfully, that I may have seen him, but what did I know of him, what did I know of his heart? But now I knew his heart, I told him. And I loved him dearly.

"I love you too, Mom," he said, "I do." But I knew he was still working on figuring it all out.

It would be the family's dogs, first Barker then Maverick, who would bring home the lessons of love, love lost and love regained. When Barker Parker died, that death had a huge impact on Dima. Dima had gotten over his initial fears of Barker, and he was often found throwing sticks for her. She was even occasionally recruited as a goalie for Dima and his friends' makeshift, sandlot soccer games. She was, however, a goalie of last resort, since she not only blocked the ball from reaching the goal, but also often ran off with it.

Barker was getting on in years, though, almost seventy in

people years, and lately had developed some serious health problems, including congestive heart failure. She could no longer fetch sticks and run up and down the back hill. I came out one morning onto the patio and saw Dima patting Barker gently, her head on his lap. There was a ball nearby that had been left outside, and suddenly Barker caught a glimpse of it. She raised her head off Dima's lap and dragged herself over to it. As though remembering better days, she brought the ball over to Dima and laid it on his lap. He looked at her, and, sensing the right thing to do, he gently rolled the ball a few feet away from her. It was close enough for her to laboriously make her way over to it, and victoriously capture it. She brought it back to Dima, laid her head in his lap, and thumped her tail madly as he scratched her ears. It would be only a few days after this that we would take her to the vet's office in a last ditch effort to save her, but she never made it back again.

The morning Barker died, she was at the animal hospital and the vet called to tell me that things were irreversible; she wasn't going to recover. We arranged to come in to say good-bye. Frank was at a meeting that morning so the children and I went in and patted Barker and talked gently to her. Barker looked up at me plaintively, then looked around, as though she were looking for Frank.

"Daddy's coming later," I said. "He'll be here later."

I swear she closed her eyes and looked more peaceful after I said that. And, indeed, she hung on for several more hours until Frank came to the office. He took her on his lap and she died in his arms a few minutes later.

"How did she know to wait for me?" he asked.

"Mom told her," Dima said, matter-of-factly.

But although we all missed Barker terribly, Dima seemed to have the most trouble. He would often say to me, "When I think of Barker, my heart hurts, Mom. I mean it really hurts, physically. I don't like losing someone I love."

"*No one does,*" I thought.

Some time after Barker died, after we had all mourned for a suitable time, we decided to bring a new puppy into our home. We went down to the local animal shelter to find one and talked with the boys about how this new puppy would become part of our family. We looked at all the little puppies in the shelter, patted them, and, finally, chose an eight-week-old wriggly black and tan dog that had just been brought in with her litter-mates. The people at the shelter gave her a bath, wrapped her in a towel, and handed her to Dima. She sat on both Dima's and Franklin's laps in the car on the way home.

Dima promptly named her Maverick, and the name turned out to be appropriate. Maverick had a wild streak and a mind of her own but she was ours, for better or worse. Unfortunately, in that early time, it turned out mostly for worse. My first clue should have been that she tried to chew the towel she was wrapped in on the way home.

During that early time with us, Maverick was a trial, to say the least. I understood that it was within the normal range of puppy behavior to chew socks and shoes. Chewing all the wallpaper off the walls, chewing a down blanket, and chewing the carpet edges was another story. And while it wasn't the normal chewing that accompanies teething, there was nothing malicious about her activities. She was anxious, high-strung beyond words. On the other hand, she was affectionate and would, unbidden, sit on your lap and lick your ear all evening. She was, as Dima put it, a good dog with bad behavior.

There even came a point in time, I shudder to admit, when in desperation I considered trying to find her a new home. Despite doggie obedience school, private training sessions, and discussions with the vet, she remained a terror. We had every chew toy on the market in her dog basket to divert her attention from the clothes and furniture, to no avail.

"You can't give her away," my husband said flatly, "no matter what. The kids think of her as a member of the family. They have to know we keep members of our family, even when they don't behave."

He had a point, although there were moments when I thought either Maverick would leave or I would. But I hung in there, and sometime later was rewarded for it. I kept my patience, threw away the destroyed items, and reassured the dog every chance I got. Gradually, her behavior began to calm down.

One day, after things had settled down, when Dima and I were folding laundry together, he said, "Well, I guess no matter what Maverick does, she will always stay with us."

"Yes, she will. After all, she's ours," I said.

He furrowed his brow. "So you mean there's nothing Maverick could do that would make us have to send her somewhere else?"

I thought about this for a minute. "Well, if she bit people we would have to do something different. We couldn't allow her to hurt anyone," I said cautiously, biting having been a sore topic in our household.

He nodded in agreement. "Oh, she would never do that. She has a good heart. She doesn't want to hurt us."

"It's true," I said.

It was a short time after that conversation that a friend had come to visit, and Dima was showing Maverick to him, instructing him on how to pat her properly. When the dog began running wildly around, grabbing things and generally misbehaving, Dima looked at the other child and said, "You know, you don't have to be perfect to be in our family. You just have to not bite."

Well put, I thought.

That night Dima told me, "I love Maverick, of course. I've had her since she was little enough to fit into the palm of my hand. But you know, I still miss Barker. My heart still hurts when I think about her."

CHAPTER 13

Strategy and Chess Moves

*As I watched my son play soccer on that crisp fall afternoon,
I knew that how he played the game was completely irrelevant. It was enough that I could keep him safe, and that I
could know his soul. As I watched the other parents yelling
instructions at their children, I realized in that moment, that
in some fundamental way, my relationship with my son had
been forged in a different press.*

My husband and Dima and Franklin had been throwing, kicking, and bouncing balls around as one of
the big bonding experiences of all the men in the family. My husband, who was in his mid-fifties, was soon looking for a little relief
from all the sustained jock activities. He wanted to leave the
extended coaching activities to men in their thirties. In our
neighborhood there were lots of quasi-organized sports activities. Baseball seemed like a natural place for us to start. Franklin
was rabidly interested in baseball, and we hoped we have both
boys play the same sport, thereby reducing the number of trips
to the game fields each week.

We signed Dima up for baseball, but as luck would have it, he was the youngest and clearly the smallest in his age group. He did look dapper, though, in his navy blue leggings, red shirt and red cap. His coaches were probably the two most understanding men in baseball history. One of them had a shortened left arm with a hand that had fewer than five fingers, and, having had to learn to compensate himself, was more than willing to make allowances for Dima's issues. The coaches made sure that if Dima got on base and made it home, they made a fuss, and even made sure that at the end of one of the practice sessions, Dima came home with a gold star on his cap, a reward for an excellent play. But despite this, Dima was not showing enthusiasm for baseball.

Finally, he came to me and said, in his solemn adult way, "Mama, if you really want me to stand there while someone throws a ball at me very hard, then I guess that's what I'll do. But think about it."

That was the last time I made him try baseball. Although Franklin continued to love, play and excel at baseball, we started Dima out in soccer. Dima had always been somewhat interested in soccer, but we had tried to dissuade him because of all the running. In baseball it's at least possible to compensate for lack of running speed by hitting the ball hard and far.

Soccer did not start off auspiciously either, despite the fact that he was determined to succeed. The first day he showed up at practice, the coach asked the children, as they came to the playing field, to drop down and do some pushups. Dima sighed, and explained to the coach in his most patient and respectful voice, "You know, I don't think that's such a good idea. See it, if I drop down on the ground, I'll get myself all dirty. I'd rather not do that." I could picture Dima's early training in a place with ninety children and no washer, dryer, or permanent press clothes, and I knew that keeping clean had been important.

The coach, not having my insight, was caught off guard for a moment. "Pardon?" he said, not sure he had heard correctly.

Dima repeated himself, still politely.

Fortunately, the coach was a man of humor and patience. "Well, we certainly couldn't have that, could we? What do you think you should do to warm up?"

I couldn't hear Dima's answer, but it was clear that he considered this carefully, and he and the coach negotiated it thoroughly.

The coach looked over Dima's head at me, as if to say, "What's with this kid? What did you do to him?"

I wanted to say what Dima always said, which was, "I didn't did it!" but I knew there was no use explaining that it wasn't my fault, that he just came that way.

The rest of Dima's soccer experience was all uphill. What he lacked in running ability, he made up for in his good use of strategy, and, of course, he had heart.

One day, Dima said to me, out of the blue, while we were riding in the car to his soccer game, "You know, I'm doing great at soccer this year. And to think, I figured I would spend my whole life in a wheelchair." He was thinking back to his early years, years in a children's hospital, years of surgery. These were times I had mostly forgotten about because by the time I knew him, he was able to walk, and he was no longer in a wheelchair.

But his words echoed through my head as I watched the soccer game that afternoon and heard the other parents yell to their children. "Get that soccer ball," they screamed. "Don't let him take it away from you, go get it!" Sometimes they yelled words of encouragement, sometimes words of frustration, but clearly they were concerned about their children's displays of agility, speed, competence.

As the game wore on and the parents huddled in groups, commenting on the plays, I stood apart. I realized in that moment, that in some fundamental way, my relationship with my son had been forged in a different press. I was awed by the fact that he could play soccer at all, and that he was here with me, connected to me. Competence was not an issue. It was enough that I could keep him safe, that I could watch him play in the grass on a crisp fall afternoon, and that I could know his soul. How he played the game was completely irrelevant. All that mattered for that moment in time was that he was mine and that he was safe.

I thought about a television special I'd seen about fathers' feelings about their relationships with their children. One father discussed his feelings about his severely retarded son, saying that he had to completely change his expectations of what fatherhood would be. He had pictured in his head those normal activities of fatherhood, such as throwing a ball, helping his son with homework, having long discussions, perhaps trading jokes. But his role as a father to his completely nonverbal son would have none of those elements. He realized he had to find completely new expectations and grapple with the meaning of his relationship to his son. He realized, over time, that his relationship became about understanding his son's soul, figuring out who he was. I understood that now.

Soccer season lasted only through the fall and we soon shifted activities. Winter evenings in upstate New York are particularly cold and dark so we were always on the lookout for interesting things to do. Franklin's grandfather had been teaching him to play chess and Franklin taught us how to play, explaining patiently to Dima how the chess pieces moved. Dima watched intently as Franklin demonstrated various moves. Dima had never played chess in Russia, but he seemed to take to it immediately.

At first, Franklin and I would play, and even at age ten he could beat me sometimes. He would plot and plan how to line up his pieces and attack at the first available moment, playing a consistently aggressive game, sometimes short on defense and sometimes a little wild. Within a short time, Dima learned the game competently enough to play competitively with Franklin. Dima seemed to grasp the idea of strategy from the very beginning, but he would sometimes be careless and miss a potentially lethal situation, and when his opponent pounced, as he invariably did, Dima would howl with rage.

"You can't take my Queen, she's mine," he would say, putting his head down in grief.

Still, despite the high tide of emotions, the chess games continued that winter. It seemed to me, a virtually non-chess playing parent, that both boys were unusually good at chess,

159

but I had no one with whom to compare them. Dima's ability to visualize anything, something we had noticed even very early on, became clearer and clearer.

One night, he and I wanted to play but had no board available.

"We can play chess anyway; just picture the board in your head. It's not all that hard!" he told me.

When I protested, "I can't do that," he looked at me sorrowfully, and said, in a disappointed tone, "Of course you can, Mama, you're just not trying hard enough."

Two other events convinced me that I was right, that both boys were good chess players. Franklin often visited his grandfather, the chess-playing, chess-teaching grandfather, on weekends. Apparently, his grandfather had a long-standing bet with any and all of the children in his family that any child who could beat him in chess would win fifty dollars. One afternoon Franklin came home, flushed with excitement and with a hundred dollars. He had beaten his grandpa in one game, won his fifty dollars, and then challenged his grandpa to a second game. His grandpa, thinking the first game was just a fluke, accepted, lost and had to cough up another fifty dollars.

Meanwhile, Dima was doggedly persisting, and improving all the time. However, it wasn't until we went to a Boy Scout jamboree that I realized he could definitely at least hold his own with children his own age.

It was late at night, the children were still up, and a group of boys began playing chess. Most were a grade or two above Dima, and played chess in a club at the school they attended. First Dima was matched up with a child about his own age, a child who he handily beat. However, in the corner there was an intense game being played, with children standing around watching every move, and rooting for one side or the other. Apparently one of the boys was the chess club champion and several grades above Dima. We watched as he skillfully set a trap, and finally maneuvered his opponent into checkmate. A roar went up! Dima would play him next since he had just won his game.

I could see Dima shifting nervously from leg to leg. I wondered how he would do. It occurred to me that the other boy was a practiced player, used to competing with other children. Besides, Dima was still so little, still such a novice at school skills that it seemed a stretch to believe he could successfully take on this competent, confident child.

To my surprise, Dima sat down at the table, looking like a professional, and didn't give away to the other children the fact that he was terribly nervous. He leaned back, introduced himself, and looked as though he'd been taking on chess players for his entire life, Paul Newman in *Cool Hand Luke*.

He drew white, which was the color he preferred to play, since white always goes first, giving that player a jump on the game. Both boys quickly set up the plastic pieces on a white and black cardboard playing board, not the green and white rolled mats I would later become familiar with in chess tournaments. Even though they had a school club, these kids were strictly recreational players. Dima took his time, setting himself up well, moving first his king's pawn, and gradually getting his power pieces in control of the board. The other boy confidently played his pieces, and quickly moved his queen out. You could tell he wasn't worried. When Dima snagged his opponent's queen early on, a rustle went through the crowd.

"Oh," said the boy with nine-year-old false bravado, "I always play better without my queen!"

Dima didn't say a word, to his credit, but he looked up at me and caught my glance. It became a slogan for us. For years to come, whenever anyone in our household was trying to put a good face on an obvious gaff, someone was sure to say, "Oh, I always play better without my queen!"

After Dima got the queen, it was all downhill for the other boy, and Dima rapidly won the game, surprising himself as much as the other child.

It wasn't until sometime later, when Dima was again attending the Saratoga Independent School that he began to play chess more seriously. Matt Witten, the father of one of the children there, regularly taught chess on Friday afternoons to any children who were interested. His own sons were excellent chess players. Dima, now with more professional coaching than Franklin or I could give him, blossomed as a chess player.

Matt encouraged him to try one of the local chess tournaments. There were apparently some very good chess players in the Saratoga area, and there were regulation tournaments set up for the children. Dima decided he'd like to give it a try.

The day of his first tournament, Frank and I brought him to the mall where it was being held, and found seats with the other parents. Dima confidently found Matt and his son, Zachary, who were already there, and waved at us, signaling he was now on his own, with the chess guys.

None of us had any idea of what to expect, our only knowledge of chess tournaments coming from the movie *Searching for Bobby Fischer*. Dima, however, was nonplussed and blithely set up his time clock as Matt had shown him how to do. Since he had never played in chess tournaments, he was in the unrated category.

After he was set up, he went over to the trophy section, and looked longingly at the inscribed trophies. He caught my eye and motioned me over to feast my eyes. There were trophies for places one through eight, and two trophies especially for unrated players.

"You think I could win one of these?" he asked. Since there were about forty children in his section, all good chess players, I didn't like his chances.

"Well, you never know. Just don't get your heart set on it. Play for the challenge in it." He gave me one of his, *yeah, right* looks, and looked back longingly at the trophy.

He was matched with another unrated player and won his first match, and went on to win three out of five matches. It was enough. By tenths of a point, he managed to win the second place trophy for unrated players. He beamed from ear to ear.

"Ma, I won one, I won one," he said, jumping up and down. He took his chess trophy and made a place of honor for it on his dresser at home. I snapped a picture of him to send back to Galina and Tatiana.

It wasn't long after that we got a totally unexpected call from Allison. When I first heard her voice, it took me by surprise, jolted me back to that first call. I couldn't imagine what she would be calling about.

CHAPTER 14

Russian Connections

When we adopted Dima in 1993, international adoption from Russia had just begun. Russia was still in political turmoil and basic necessities were in short supply. It was difficult for Russian people to make ends meet let alone travel. But within a few years of our adoption, things started to change. Russia opened up to other countries, and people came back and forth. Galina, the head of the children's home, was scheduled to come to America for a conference and she hoped to visit some of the children she had placed.. She was especially interested in visiting Dima since he was the oldest child who had traveled across the ocean to his new family, and the one she had known longest and best.

*A*fter the initial follow up period, we didn't keep in contact with Allison. Now, she told me that Galina was coming to the States and was due to arrive the next week. Allison was hoping to have her visit us because adoption officials were still interested in making sure the children went to reasonable homes, and were not being used for nefarious purposes such as child slavery.

Allison had called to make the arrangements and as usual in my dealings with Allison, everything happened impossibly quickly. I agreed to the visit, although not without some trepidation. While this was our chance to show Galina how well Dima had fared, and it was Frank's chance to meet Galina, we worried a bit about how Dima would react. Frank had missed out on seeing where Dima had lived, on knowing the people responsible for his early care, and he was intrigued with the idea of meeting Galina. After all, even though Galina wasn't a relative of Dima's, she had had the most interest in our son in his early years; she knew him, knew his background better than anyone else, and was in a sense our link to his history. She was the one who had memories of him in his first pair of little red glasses, of giving him a tissue to hold against his gum when a tooth fell out.

But even more than that, Galina held the key to the future of scores of other children. When Dima came to this country, he really was a pioneer of sorts. International adoption of Russian children by Americans began in the fall of 1992, with a relatively small number of children being allowed out. So when Dima was adopted just a few months later, in March 1993, this was still very new and there was a political uproar over the concept in Russia. Were the children safe, were they being treated well, and of course, were they adjusting? The answers to these questions would be the basis of decisions being made about adoption law, and Dima was one of those children in the forefront.

In the beginning, I frequently got calls for pictures of him, hopefully pictures that would show him well fed, well dressed and well taken care of. The officials in Russia were scrutinizing the information coming back from America, trying to make decisions about what should be done about international adoption. And even now, after a couple of years had elapsed, Galina realized, I'm sure, the import of her decisions, and I wanted her to know that things had turned out well for Dima.

Having Galina visit in some way also connected me to my own roots and the immigrant experience. I was riding in the wave of an historic point in time, although initially I was unaware of the extent of the implications.

Through my adoption of Dima, I began to understand more about the immigrant experience and understand it differently than I previously did. When I was a young child, I had imagined my ancestors coming here, one by one, standing alone in a strange country, not knowing the language, and being completely isolated.

Perhaps I imagined this because it was so romantic a story for me, or perhaps I imagined it because I was given to reading novels about young women who lived through difficult times, women sent to relatives they didn't know, sent away during the war. In any event, when I imagined a person emigrating from one country to another, I always pictured them in my mind's eye as being terribly alone and isolated. I was amazed at my relative's fortitude and courage, and often wondered if I would have fallen short under the same daunting conditions.

I didn't realize until later that many people immigrated with friends or families, or, if they immigrated alone, they were on their way to see relatives. The difficult task for many was to make sense of a culture which relied on different assumptions, to be able to grasp the similarities and differences, to understand the subtleties of a society that operated at once differently and the same.

However, in the beginning Dima seemed to be that lone, isolated pioneer of my imaginings. He did not come here with a group of familiar Russian speaking children, nor did he come to join such a group. He was a lone pioneer, sent into a foreign group of people, people he didn't know and couldn't understand. His job was to survive, and to adapt wholly to his new culture. It was a challenge few people have faced throughout history, and even fewer children, although I'm sure that there have always been children who suffered similar dislocations, although usually in times of war or natural catastrophes.

As I tried to connect Dima with Russians hoping to give him some sense of familiarity, some sense of community and continuity, I realized during that early time that his feelings went through shifts: shifts in identity, and loyalty, a confusion of trying to understand where he fit in. He had a foot in two very different worlds. There were tremendous, but often subtle, differences in the cultural views of bringing up children, differences that Dima even as a young child felt.

I can remember one day talking with a close Russian friend of mine, a women named Yelena. I told her that I was taking Dima for swimming lessons, to "see if he liked it." I often approached activities casually, with the typical American philosophy that it was good for children to try things, to explore a variety of skills and find where their talents and interests lay.

Yelena looked at me, dumbfounded for a minute, then laughed. "Ah, it is such a different way," she said, quietly. "In Russia, when you decide your children must take swimming lessons, you bring them to the swim coach, and the swim coach makes sure they learn, and it must be the right way. They must work as hard as possible. The swim coach will not tolerate any nonsense, any dawdling. It would be a waste of her time, and a waste of the parents' money. The children must take the lessons seriously."

"Oh," I said, somewhat chastened. But Yelena had smiled and given me a hug, showing me our friendship far transcended any parenting differences. I could recruit Yelena to help me with this visit from Galena, to translate, if nothing else.

This would also be my chance to find out the answers to questions that had long lingered. There were so many things I wanted to know, to understand, questions I had not thought to ask the first time around. I wanted to know where Dima's cross had come from, and I wanted to know what had happened to Nadia and to the others. I would have to wait patiently now, just a little longer.

But first I would have to prepare Dima.

"Dima, you know we often have company, visitors," we said, as Dima sat on the floor playing with his Lego blocks.

"Uh huh," he answered vaguely.

"Well, this time you are going to have a special visitor. Remember Galina, from Russia? She is coming to visit-to say hello. She has to come to this country for a meeting and would love to see you."

Dima continued playing with his Legos, not even looking up.

I tried again. "You remember Galina, from Russia. She's coming here. Isn't that exciting?"

He continued playing with his Legos. "I know who she is Mama. I'm not stupid."

"Well, we'll be picking her up at the train station next week. You can come with us. That's always your favorite place to go." And it was. He was always thrilled to go pick up relatives who arrived by train to see us. He was the original planes, trains and automobiles, guy. If it moved, he was there.

This time he looked up. "I'm not going to the train station. It's fine if she wants to come here and 'hello' me. She can even stay here. But you and Daddy will have to pick her up. I'm not going."

I had worried about his reaction to seeing her, but his reaction to going to the train station took me by surprise. I thought he might be disconcerted by faces from the past popping up, but I never thought he worried about being taken away, or God forbid, being sent back. All those fears were long gone, I hoped, and had died after that time period when he worried that you could exchange a bad child for a better one. Maybe those fears never die. All I know was that no amount of reassurance convinced him to go to the train station.

The evening Galina was to arrive, Frank got ready to meet her. The station was way downtown, not someplace I liked to drive at night. Frank casually mentioned that if Dima accompanied him, it would help him to recognize Galina. Dima looked at the darkening sky and told us it was way too late for him and he had to be in his pajamas. So, for the first time ever in our history, Dima took a shower and got into his pajamas without being asked. The only glitch was that it was about two hours before his normal bedtime. *Nyet* train station for him. We looked at each other and shrugged.

Frank headed off to the station to pick up Galina alone, hoping there weren't too many other middle-aged white haired women in Russian attire at the depot. Frank found her without difficulty and brought her home to see all of us. Dima looked adorable in his pajamas, with his wet hair slicked back, fresh from the shower.

Galina was very excited to see him, but he was shy, and although he was polite, he acted as though he didn't know her. Galina came with big packages, the famous Russian gifts. She offered Dima a beautifully wrapped, colorful package.

"For me?" he asked. He was used to seeing Galina as the somewhat distant head of the children's home, a person who gave directions, who supervised procedures. He was not used to seeing her come bearing him fancy gifts. Obviously his status in the world had changed.

He opened the gift and both he and I gasped in amazement. In the box were ten wooden hand-carved Russian soldiers, the old- fashioned kind you might expect to see in a production of the *Nutcracker Suite*, when the toy soldiers came to life.

Dima turned them over and over, examining the carving, appreciating their beauty. He then ran into his room and set them up on one of his shelves, smiling and proclaiming, as usual, "Dima's."

But still, even after this, Dima continued to hang back. He didn't speak Russian anymore, and although he probably still understood some of the language, when Galina tried to speak to him in Russian, the only language she knew, he shied away.

One time she got him off in the corner by himself, and I heard her asking him, using the few English words she had, if he was happy. "Are you happy?" she kept repeating when he ignored her. I'm sure that that was the question that haunted her.

I had arranged for Yelena to come over the next day in order to translate for us. I had hoped there would be a time when I could finally get the missing pieces of Dima's history, could get answers for all those questions I'd had. In the meantime, I had few words in common so I relied on our old standby: family pictures. I had Dima drag out our big box of pictures and snuggle down next to me, while I showed them to Galina who looked on and smiled broadly.

There were pictures of Dima on skis, Dima swimming in the pool, Dima on his bicycle. When we got to the picture of Dima with his class, Galina put her hand on mine to stop me from flipping to the next picture and asked me something. I couldn't understand what she wanted to know after several attempts, she gave up and motioned that she'd like to hold on to the picture. I nodded, and she slipped the picture into her purse.

The next morning I made a big pot of coffee and when Yelena arrived I had planned to have everyone sit around our breakfast table. I had hoped Dima would sleep late as he usually did, but of course that morning he was up at dawn. The only place to talk out of earshot was on the patio, and it was uncharacteristically cold that August morning. I remember the three of us sitting out there, wrapped in sweaters, shivering, impatient to finish the conversation and go back inside where it was warm. I felt disappointed that the easy relaxed conversation I had hoped for was not to be. But still, I could cram in a few hastily asked questions.

I asked Galina about Dima's legendary stubbornness. I had wondered if he had always been that way, or if all the changes, the differences in language, in homes had irrevocably affected him.

"Oh," she said, "he was always that way, but always so helpful. He would get so frustrated that the other children would not properly clean up and he would be there with a sponge, cleaning the table after an art project. But stubborn!" Then she added, "But all the children there are stubborn. It is a characteristic of the region. All the people are very stubborn. They are known for this."

"And what about his cross, the one he wore around his neck, tied with a shoelace? Where did he get it from?" I asked. I held my breath. I had always hoped that it wasn't a gift given to him by a mother who parted tearfully from him. I couldn't bear that somehow. And yet, I knew it must have been difficult for a parent to give him up, cross or no cross. Of course, I didn't know the reasons, nor the degree of anguish his parents felt; all that would have to remain a mystery.

"Ah," said Galina, "the cross. I brought in a priest to bless all the children. And he gave crosses to the older children, the ones who could understand. Dima was very interested in this, and asked many questions. And he wore his cross always, on a shoe lace around his neck."

Still, I breathed a sigh of relief. Then Galina put her hand on mine for a moment, to signal that she had something to ask. She reached into her purse and pulled out the picture of Dima in his little class of fifteen children and his enthusiastic-looking teacher.

"Ah," said Yelena, "she wants to know about this picture, this group of children."

I explained that it was his class, and I could see a look of pleasure, of surprise cross her face.

"So few children in American classes?" she asked, looking at the group of fifteen or so children standing together, smiling at the camera.

"It is a private school. It has smaller classes." I said.

She nodded. "He got so little attention in his early years. Now, he will have more in school, he will catch up. Good."

I thought about that momentarily. If there is one thing Dima had in his new life it was attention. But catch up? No, I thought to myself slowly, that's not it. Catching up implies that one is on the same road, but behind the pack. Dima's not really behind at all I thought; he's on a different path than most people, perhaps the famous path less traveled. His reading had come along, painfully at first, but gradually, gradually, it was falling into place.

"You know, Mama," he had told me, when he was a little older, "I can read now. I really can." Then he sighed, "Now the problem is writing." I had smiled. It was always something.

I looked at Galina but didn't say anything aloud. Instead I squeezed her hand and gave her the picture envelope.

I had more questions, but it was so cold, everyone was eager to get inside. I started to ask about the scar on his chin, and I had yet to ask about Nadia, but I could see Galina shifting from side to side, pulling her thin sweater more tightly around her. Still, I asked about Nadia and about the other children. She shrugged, and spoke matter-of-factly to Yelena. Yelena told me gently, putting her hand on mine.

"She thinks Nadia lives in town, in the home for older children. She had hepatitis B, you know, and she wasn't eligible for adoption overseas. But perhaps someone there will take care about her future." I have since heard of children with hepatitis B being adopted internationally, so I don't know the whole story, but perhaps from that region it wasn't allowed.

Galina rose to go inside, and I knew manners dictated that I must let her go. Once we went back into the house, Dima came looking for me, and I knew it was the end of any private conversation.

Dima seemed a bit edgier, a bit crankier than usual, although not different in any definable way. I put my arms around his shoulders for a moment. I wondered if Galina had heard of the problems many of the children had in adjusting to their families, the lack of connection that plagued some of them. I hoped she knew we loved him, that we treated him well.

I saw Galina shake her head and sigh, not entirely approving as she watched me talking, coaxing Dima, and then I realized I was caught up in another of those defining moments, those times when I knew my view was only a sliver of the realities that existed. Galina shrugged and said she didn't understand the way Americans disciplined their children. They were too lenient, too indulgent. She told me, through Yelena's translations, that she watched a mother with a child at the train station. The child was acting up and the mother was putting up with it. Americans spoiled the children, she thought. So perhaps Russians didn't entirely approve of the culture, of the way their children would be raised, but still, I could feel her relief to know he was safe.

That night Galina spent time with the family. Both children busied themselves by sitting on the couch, Franklin reading aloud to Dima. It was hard to believe, but no one was fighting this last night, no imaginary toy bombs were exploding, and no little green men were falling out of cabinets. I looked with pride at the family we had built.

When Galina left the next day, with her pocketbook stuffed with photographs, Dima and I waved goodbye to her from the doorstop. He never did go to the train station, but he smiled broadly as he yelled, "Bye, bye, Galina."

That evening, long after supper was over, Dima and my husband went out onto the front deck to sit together companionably in the dark of night. It was an unusually clear night, and the two of them admired the stars, which were highly visible against the black sky. Dima got up after a while, stood quietly next to my husband, draping an arm over his shoulder. "You know," he said, after a while, awe in his voice, "when I look at all those stars in the sky I think of all the children in the world needing homes. And I think about how lucky I am."

My husband couldn't say a word. He just put his arm around Dima and pulled him in tighter, amazed at Dima's insight.

Epilogue

Between 1993 and 2010, about 45 thousand children were adopted from Russia.[19] *Perhaps because of the large number of children coming out of Europe at one time, or the new ability of people to connect with one another through the internet, common problems and patterns began to emerge. The need for research on the effects of early neglect and the need for better training and support for adoptive parents became evident.*

*D*ima and Franklin are both now adults. Dima still watches me like a hawk and picks up anything I may have forgotten or left behind-the memory of the glove incident never far away, but he has grown to appreciate my steadfastness and honesty, and to trust me.

Despite his early problems with hip dysplasia, and the early worries by the orphanage staff that he might never walk, he not only walks, but is a terrific skier and ski instructor. Sometimes as I watch him go out with his skis over his shoulder I think of how amazed Galina would be to see him now. He is bright, and insightful, with a sense of humor, but as many children with his background do, he struggled for years with reading and related issues, although he has largely overcome them at this point. He has completed his associate's degree and seems to be on his way to doing something interesting with his life. And, most important to me, he is kind, caring, and cared for, and he still amazes me with his insights. Franklin has remained the calm person he has always been and has done exceptionally well in school and in his job. Dima and Franklin are close and have overcome all that initial sibling rivalry!

Dima's early years of living in clinics and orphanages and his numerous surgical procedures affected him, but the effects were not always what one would expect. He never had the attachment issues so prevalent in the stories of international adoption, but he is careful before trusting people, he watches body language, and how people behave. In some ways he is more attuned than the average young person to the nuances of relationships.

Life also changed for the people we met in Russia. I got a telephone call from Galina's daughter, Masha one day, years ago. She was studying at a university in the United States and spoke fluent English. Not only did Masha have e-mail, but in Syktyvkar, at the orphanage, there was e-mail. Although no one in Syktyvkar spoke English, it was possible for me to e-mail Masha, have her translate it and e-mail Galina, and vice versa. I thought of how years ago Syktyvkar seemed like the ends of the earth to me, how isolated I felt when I visited there. Now, I could communicate in an instant. I sent a picture of Dima to them via the Internet, and they were able to receive it seconds later! I heard later that the orphanage is now closed because of funding difficulties and that the children there were moved to other places.

Our personal story is just one small part of the story of adoption. International adoption from Russia, which began in 1992, has been overhauled several times, with changes in the procedures and in the requirements. There were 15 children adopted from Russia who died in the United States between 1996 and 2010 as a result of actions by their adoptive parents. Authorities in Russia and in adoption agencies in the

United States began to look more closely at the underlying issues and consider ways to better protect children adopted internationally. There was a virtual freeze on adoptions from Russia in 2007 which resulted in the re-accreditation of a select few adoption agencies that were allowed to continue to operate.[20] In 2008, The Hague Adoption Convention, a multilateral treaty designed to bring certain protections to internationally adopted children, birth parents and adoptive parents, was enacted. This brought changes to the adoption world, and in the U.S., it included mandatory training for parents. The training involved explanations of common physical and emotional conditions of orphans, and preparation for the challenges that often come with adopting a child from an institutional setting. In 2010 a freeze was again called for when 7- year-old Arytom Sarelyev/Justin Hansen was sent back to Russia, on a plane, alone, with a note pinned to his coat by adoptive mother The note basically said that she could no longer care for him due to his behavior and that the information she had gotten about him prior to adoption was false. The Russian Foreign Minister called it the "last straw" in dealing with adoptions from the United States. Although there was a temporary suspension in international adoption, and a huge outcry and investigation, adoption from Russia did continue.

There have been changes in which children can be adopted, and which parents can adopt. When inter-country adoption from Russia began, only children with special needs were allowed to be adopted internationally. That changed so that children without special needs could also be adopted internationally, but documented efforts had to be made to place them first with Russian families. There have been changes in procedures for home studies and for training for prospective parent. The political aspects of international adoption are complex and involve money, resources, cultural views as well as the necessity of understanding the developmental issues involved.

ENDNOTES

[1] Lubit, Roy, J. Martin Maldonado-Duran, Linda Helmig Bram. "Child Abuse and Neglect, Reactive Attachment Disorder." *Medicine.* 10 14, 2009. http://emedicine.medscape.com/article/915447 - overview.

[2] Craft, Carrie. "Russian Adoption Murders." 08 03, 2005. http://About.Com:Adoption/FosterCare (accessed 02 03, 2011).

[3] Hage, Deborah. "Older Child Adoption Does NOT= AttachmentDisorder." *Rainbow Kids.* 12 01, 2008.http://www.rainbowkids.com (accessed 03 01, 2011).

[4] Caspi, A., Sugden, K., Moffitt, T. E., Taylor, A., Craig, I. W., Harrington, H., et al. "Influence of life stress on depression: Moderation by polymorphism in the 5HTT gene." *Science 301(5631),* 2003: 386-389.

[5] Skeels, Harold M. "Mental Development of Children in Foster Homes." *Journal of Cognitive Psychology* 2 1938: 33-43.

[6] Lifton, Betty Jean. *Journey of the Adopted Self.* Basic Books, Harper Collins, 1995.

[7] Restak, Richard. *The Secret Life of the Brain.* Washington, D.C.: The Dana Press and The Joseph Henry Press, 2001, 24-25.

[8] Restak, Richard. *The Secret Life of the Brain*. Washington, D.C.: The Dana Press and The Joseph Henry Press, 2001, 22-24.

[9] Sapolsky, Robert. *Biology and Human Behavior: The Neurological Origins of Individuality Part 2 of 2nd edition. 2*. Vol. 2. Chantilly, Virginia: The Teaching Company, 2005.

[10] Bowlby, J. *Attachment and Loss vol. 1*. London: Hogarth, 1969.

[11] Lubit, Roy, J. Martin Maldonado-Duran, Linda Helmig Bram. Child Abuse and Neglect, Reactive Attachment Disorder." *Medicine*. 10 14, 2009. http://emedicine.medscape.com/article/915447 - overview.

[12] Cogan, Patty. *Parenting Your Internationally Adopted Child*. Cambridge Mass: Harvard Common Press, 2008.

[13] Gindis, Boris, FRUA New Yorkers, vol.3 issue 2 Winter 2003.

[14] Foley, Yuchon Chen and Mullis, F. 2008. "Interpreting Children's Figure drawings:Basic Guidelines for the School Counselor." *Georgia School Counselor Association Journal* 1(1) 28-37.

[15] Koppitz, Elizabeth. *Psychological Evaluation of Children's Human Figure Drawings*. Grune and Stratton,1968.

[16] Foley, Yuchon Chen and Mullis, F. 2008. "Interpreting Children's Figure drawings:Basic Guidelines for the School Counselor." *Georgia School Counselor Association Journal* 1(1) 28-37.

[17] Restak, Richard. *The Secret Life of the Brain*. Washington, D.C.: The Dana Press and The Joseph Henry Press, 2001, 56-58.

[18] Carter, Rita. *The Human Brain*. London, New York, Melbourne, Munich, Delhi: Dotling Kindersley, 2009, 151.

[19] "Adoption Institute:International Adoption Facts." *Adoption Institute*. http://www.adoptioninstitute.org/FactOvervies/international.html (accessed 11 8, 2010).

[20] Osborne, Martha. "The future of International Adoption. " *Rainbow Kids* 2008 http://www.rainbowkids.com

CPSIA information can be obtained at www.ICGtesting.com
Printed in the USA
LVOW131954270812

296204LV00001B/8/P